EVEN WITHOUT IRENE

An Autobiography

ROBERT GREACEN

D1420296

LAGAN PRESS
BELFAST
1995

Published by
Lagan Press
PO Box 110 BT12 4AB, Belfast

The publishers wish to acknowledge the financial assistance
of the Arts Council of Northern Ireland in the production of this book.

A catalogue record of this book is available from the British Library

ISBN: 1 873687 51 6
Author: Greacen, Robert
Title: Even Without Irene
Subtitle: An Autobiography
Format: Paperback (130 mm x 198 mm)
1995

Front Cover: *City Hall Under Snow* by William Conor (c 1925)
(Courtesy of the estate of William Conor and the Ulster Museum)
Cover Design by December Publications
Set in New Baskerville
Printed by Noel Murphy, Belfast

for
Roy McFadden
—friend and poet

My son used to say: 'Whatever oppresses a man must be wrought out in another medium' and when he himself suffered any ill, he made a poem out of it.

—J.W. Goethe's mother

CONTENTS

ONE

The Londonderry Air

Mother's name was Elizabeth and, like the mother of John the Baptist, she was over forty when her first and only child, myself, was born. The date was October 24th, 1920. Many years later, when I started to work for the United Nations Association in London, I was told that October 24th was the most important date in their year—United Nations Day. My life has been associated with 'foreigners'. I spent much of it teaching English as a foreign language.

The name of the city I was born in is disputed. At the time of my birth it was called Londonderry. Now the majority of its people simply call it Derry. If people in Ireland ask me where I was born I can, if wishing to be politic, say 'The Maiden City' or use the more recent coinage, 'Stroke City'.

I was delivered by a Dr. McCurdy. Of that gentleman I know nothing else, but, to me at least, his name is blessed except in fits of depression. It seems I was not expected to live, but I have always delighted in confounding the expectations of others. Father came from further south in Ulster, Co. Monaghan. My natal year saw the start of partition when the island of Ireland was divided into Northern Ireland and what, for some years, was called the Irish Free State.

As every Irish schoolboy knows, or used to know, Derry/ Londonderry is often referred to as the 'Maiden City' because of

11

the fight for survival of the Protestant inhabitants during James II's siege in 1689. G.M. Trevelyan, the great historian, wrote: "The burghers of Londonderry endured the famous siege, facing starvation in the spirit that the citizens of Haarlem and Leyden had shown in like case against the Spaniard."

The city—whatever name you care to give it—was and is a place steeped in tradition and continuity. Even today, one finds there readily enough a reminder of the brutal facts of history—the walls that have been celebrated in ballads, the River Foyle that leads to the ancient city on the hill and the two cathedrals, not to speak of the British Army presence.

History—or what passes for history—for the Irish has a reality that can be frightening and which can perpetuate ancient feuds. As a boy, from my aunts and mother I heard many a story of the suffering endured by the defiant Protestant citizenry, and in language no less eloquent than that of Trevelyan. I heard of the so-called traitor Lundy who had the same significance for us as Quisling for Norwegians during the Second World War. These tales of heroism and stoic endurance were, it was true, told me in Belfast to which my family had moved. Derry indeed was in decline. The Protestants were moving east as the city became more and more populated by Catholics. But even in true-blue, loyalist Belfast, the hearts of my mother and her sisters were still in the Maiden City of their youth when their lives had centred round the Presbyterian Church in Carlisle Road.

Derry for them—they said 'Derry' in conversation but used 'Londonderry' officially—meant Protestant Derry. History meant Protestant history. Suffering and heroism meant that undergone by Protestants. There was never a whisper of the sixth century Derry that had become a great centre of missionary zeal, long before we Scots-Irish had settled there—along with some English—sword in one hand and Bible in the other.

Nobody told me of Colmcille who founded a monastery on the hill over-looking the wide tidal river. Nobody spoke of how, in 563, now named St. Columba, he created a great Christian settlement in Iona, so spreading the Gospel through pagan

12

Scotland and northern England. Nor did I know of how Irish monks brought Christianity to western Europe after the fall of Rome and of how the saint wrote of his beloved place:

Were all the tributes of Scotia mine,
From the midland to its borders,
I would give all for one little cell
In my beautiful Derry.

No, not a syllable of all that history was uttered, for the very good reason that my mother and aunts knew nothing of it. Theirs, I repeat, was the Protestant version of history—the near-disaster of the 105-day siege before the boom was broken and ships sailed up the Foyle with food for the gallant Protestants. And of course they were gallant and determined, but no more exclusively in the right than their opponents. The past in Ireland, especially in the north, hangs round people's necks like a gigantic albatross.

None of us could foretell that history had not finished with the Protestant city which was so rapidly turning into an Irish Catholic city. Nobody guessed that one day this place would erupt violently, that television would bring names like Creggan and Bogside into English living rooms. It could not be foreseen that on January 30th, 1972, British paratroopers would shoot dead 13 Catholics and that this 'Bloody Sunday' would lead to the burning down of the British Embassy in Dublin. History, God knows, has scourged Ireland for centuries. The pity of it is that it has struck so frequently at elegant, beautiful Derry.

As a boy, I often had to listen to the praise of things past and people long dead. What, I used to wonder, had it to do with me? I was interested in sex and Hollywood movies, not in all these old wives' tales of conflict. My aunts and mother might have been talking of the early Christians being thrown to the lions for all I cared. Their anecdotes of their own early lives I found just as boring. Now they, too, have passed into history and it is too late for me to take notes.

What can I remember of those first five or so years of my life in Derry? I can see myself at the age of three or four, in the early 1920s, standing in Bennett Street, where Dr. McCurdy had delivered me, looking through my legs at a fascinatingly topsy-turvy world. Another image of myself is of stroking a grey horse that pulled a bread cart, and marvelling at the size and beauty of the animal, and wanting yet fearing to touch its smartly-groomed tail.

I recall, too, being taught to say 'Logan's Loaf' and rendering it as 'Ogan's Oaf' to an amused feminine audience. 'L' and 'r' were as difficult for me to master as they proved for Japanese students I was to teach several decades later. I used to proclaim my name, with some pride, as 'Lobelt'. I was taught a few simple Bible stories and I think the hope existed that this only child might one day feel 'the call' to the Presbyterian ministry. These stories I was encouraged to repeat in my lisping accents and I soon realised that a storyteller can capture and hold an audience.

I was particularly addicted to the story of Moses, with variations on the theme. The Old Testament for us was as real, perhaps even more so, than the New. Jews were respected as the people of the Book, not thought of with contempt or hatred. So it proved that bulrushes, wilderness, rock, children of Israel, were colourful props for an exhibitionistic little boy. I liked to emphasise the length and tedium of Moses' journey using repetition—"… and he go-ed and he go-ed". This, I sensed, would bring the house down.

How many years I spent in Derry I cannot accurately remember, but an old directory lists my grandmother's name until 1925, so I think it must have been five. I have not forgotten, however, the sensation of being, as I believed, deserted by my parents and left in the care of my maternal granny and her two daughters. I cried bitterly for my mother. When I asked for her, granny said: "She's gone away for a wee while."

"Where? Where?"

"To a big, big city called Belfast."

"What for?"

"To earn pennies for her Robbie."

This news was not comforting. It alarmed me, saddened me. I felt betrayed. It was as if the sky had fallen on my head. It could not be. She could not have left me. Nothing would console me, not even the grey horse to which I once delighted to feed lumps of sugar. Nor the recital of that story about some old Jew called Moses. No, I did not want granny or my two aunts—kind and loving though they were.

Aunt Annie begged me to look at the man in the moon. Man in the moon, indeed! Had I but known the words, what obscenities I would have uttered! But small children know only the language of yells and sobs. They know betrayal, too. The parting, as it happened, was not final by any means, yet the relationship with mother never fully recovered. She lived to be nearly ninety and we were on loving terms—and yet ...

Time and again, I have made an effort to re-establish the early sense of harmony, oneness, completeness. Time and again, I have endeavoured to re-enter the lost paradise. Is it like catching a soap bubble and holding it in one's hand? The Belfast novelist, Forrest Reid, the first writer I ever met, put forward in his autobiography, *Apostate*, the suggestion that a certain kind of creative artist finds his motivation in discontent, so that, as Reid puts it, "his art is a kind of crying for Elysium". He may well have revealed the reason why, as a grown man, I have felt the necessity to write poems. Poetry is the antidote for hurt and frustration.

But I often think back to those Derry days. Aunt Annie, kind soul then and in later years, apart from attempting to make me believe in the reality of the man in the moon—a ploy I stubbornly resisted—used to take me out for what she called 'air'. She could ameliorate yet not dissolve the bitterness in my infant heart. The giants of the adult world, I felt, were not to be trusted. Kindness might mask betrayal.

Throughout my life, when I hear the bitter-sweet strains of the 'Londonderry Air'—as haunting a melody as has ever come out of Ireland, north or south—I think of my native city and of being taken out for 'air'. I recall with affection, not unmixed perhaps with some shame, of this good aunt of mine and her long perambulations with a fractious, self-willed, dreamy little boy along Shipquay Street and the Waterside. And I have sometimes wondered how my life would have turned out had I spent my boyhood on the banks of the River Foyle in Colmcille's 'beautiful Derry'.

TWO

Where the Wild Thyme Blows

A golden-curled girl of eleven took me by the hand to St. Simon's
School in Belfast's Donegall Road and so introduced me to
'education'. After a short sojourn in paradise—being coddled
by the golden-haired girl and moulding plasticine—I was, for
some reason, abruptly despatched to a school at the top of
Broadway ruled by a Mr. McDougall. Here, there were tough
boys around and no golden-haired girls. I feared the worst but
do not remember being bullied. I remember singing for the first
time 'Rock of Ages' and having no idea what it was about, being
in particular puzzled by the phrase 'cleft for me'. I only knew
that the hymn had something to do with Christianity.

Mr. Taylor, a pleasant young man, was my teacher. Aunt
Tillie—now I was living with my two aunts who ran a shop at the
corner of Broadway and the Donegall Road—used to wake me
in the morning and hurry me out of bed with the words:

Ding-a-ling-a-ling, the old school bell,
Mr. Taylor's up to say that all is well.

Or else she would greet me with the verse:

Get up lazy Robert, get up lazy Rob,
The sun through your window is shining.

17

If you only but knew, it is saying to you
Time's precious, don't waste it in dreaming!

I remember watching older and daring boys walk across a parapet over the Blackstaff river which flowed along a few doors from the corner house. Another memory is of using a net and putting tiny fish into a glass jam jar, and then of falling into the river and being hauled out again.

My grandmother, whose maiden name had been Smyth and who had been brought up in Co. Tyrone, was a tight-laced, black-clad, at times stern, at times kindly, old body who lived contentedly and God-fearingly with her two daughters, my aunts. She and they prayed for guidance, for they had no men to look after them and my father only posed problems for them. They all believed in honesty, hard work, thrift. Holidays were unknown, not even a half-day at the nearby seaside town of Bangor. Yet cheerfulness prevailed.

Then mother and father appeared once more and claimed their boy. I cried and asked to stay with granny and the two aunts, but I had to go. That meant a move to the country when I was somewhere between eight and nine, in the last years of the 1920s. This mysterious and forbidding place, 'the country', proved to be a farm about three or four miles from the town of Castleblayney in Co. Monaghan. We went across the border into what was then called the Free State. Even so, we were still in the historic province of Ulster where Protestant influence, though declining, was still fairly strong.

A few miles outside Castleblayney, on the way to Ballybay, my Aunt Liz-Ann, a widow, ran a hill farm with the help of her brother George, who owned a near-by farm. An adjoining farm had been taken by my father who, tired of fortune-hunting in the big city, had decided to try his hand at the rural pursuits of his ancestors. He never really liked farming, however, and I often heard him speak contemptuously of the back-breaking effort that, in the end, brought little reward other than rheumatism and bankruptcy. Still, he had ventured forth, probably on the

18

advice of his brothers and sister, and with the insurance money he had received when his Belfast shop had burned down. Back to the plough and the cart and the dung heap, if not to the plough and the stars, in the county of little fields and lakes whose stony soil would be the inspiration of the poet Patrick Kavanagh.

Father was a restless man. He wanted quick results. His reach tended to exceed his grasp. When disappointed, he turned to the whiskey bottle rather than to the Bible for comfort. This dismayed both his own family and mother's, except that his own kin found excuses for him: "Harry suffers from his nerves ... that's what it is. He needs a tonic." Mother's family made more abrasive comments, for granny had been against him from the beginning and advised mother not to marry him. I think he was over-sensitive and under-confident. He kept hoping that his day would come but it never did. He gradually slid down the social and economic scale.

I cannot remember as much I would like about these far-off days in the late 1920s when father ploughed and hoed and swore and kept pigs. I was sent to a shack-like country school where I was the only Protestant and excused prayers on that account—much to my satisfaction. On one occasion, I fell on top of a pile of sharp stones and cut my knee so that there is still a scar on it. I always had shoes to wear, but I envied those hardy lads who walked through field and bog and over uneven road surfaces in their bare feet. They were tough and, like all boys, I admired toughness. I never found any hostility because of my minority religion. I sensed a difference from the others without quite knowing why it existed.

We had a cat called Polly and Aunt Liz-Ann had a collie named Victor. I loved both cat and dog. One window of our house was edged with bits of coloured glass and this seemed to me extremely grand. Father beat me once, hitting me round the head, for bad handwriting, having tried to 'teach' me in his own amateur fashion. I fell to the floor sobbing and I think it was then that the bitterness I felt for him began. For years we were to clash. Father represented authority simply because he was older. I

19

started to resent authority, but had the sense to conceal my hostility. The injustice of the world began to impinge.

It may possibly be too fanciful to suppose that Father's sneer at my inability to 'write' set up a process of over-compensation that made me determine, a few years later, to become a professional writer, come what may. Certainly, at that period the relationship with father had not deteriorated to the extent where I consciously wished to kill him and have mother all to my self. Under the surface of polite obedience of course that is precisely what I *did* want. He sensed it, I suppose, and only used my inability to 'write' as a rationalisation of his jealousy. Often he would tell me that my teachers had complained to him of my 'stupidity' and lack of concentration. If so, they gave me no sign of their displeasure.

The lilac at Aunt Liz-Ann's enchanted me as did the army of spring daffodils in Uncle George's semi-wild garden. My aunt was kind and chatty, Uncle George was kind and silent, but loved playing practical jokes. Asked by my aunt if he intended tackling a particular job the next day, he would be silent for a long time. Then he would answer in a monosyllable—ay or no. At times I could not help wishing that Uncle George had been my father. Children know what adults to like, just as they know which animals to trust. I trusted Uncle George's collie, Victor, and I hoped he trusted me, though sometimes I teased him. I longed to trust my father, but somehow sixth-sensed it would be a mistake.

After nearly a year in the country, mother and I went to visit mother's relatives in Belfast. That was a pleasant expedition to a formerly well-known feminine world, a world of security and affection that I had lost. Not a detail of that visit stands out, for happiness leaves no trace on the map of memory.

But the time came to return to Castleblayney. There we hired a car for the journey home. The familiar lanes came in sight, fresh and clean-smelling after the chimney smoke of the city. When our house came into view, mother burst into tears, then sobs. She took me in her arms. "Robbie," she began. "Robbie ..."

I looked out of the car, focused my short-sighted brown eyes on a blackened skeleton. Our home had been burned down! I felt numb, tearless with apprehension and excitement.

Some of the furniture had been saved and taken up the hill to Aunt Liz-Ann's, where we all stayed while father debated the next move. I wondered if he had started the fire himself. In imagination, I could see his lean figure sprinkling petrol from a can. Then I could see him strike the match that started the great blaze. Polly had disappeared, burned to death perhaps. I cried for the cat I loved, not for our homelessness.

Weeks passed and one day father received what was described as a 'big cheque'. The bigger the sum of money, the bigger the cheque, I supposed. Memory may be playing a trick on me, but I recall the actual sum as being £600. I heard a neighbour remark, "Harry's on the pig's back now". Flushed with triumph, father appeared in a roseate hue as an organiser of victory. To me, he seemed a prince of fire-raisers but, of course, I may be quite wrong. I wanted to ask him if he had started the fire, but was afraid to mention the subject. The witnesses all died many years ago and the secret—assuming there was a secret—is buried with them.

We were soon to hear about the next venture, a new business in Belfast. Back again to the city of red trams and slogan-daubed walls and shipyard gantries and the sad hooting of ships' sirens. Father explained that farming was dirty, back-breaking work, fit only for the unambitious. Now he had the greatest idea of modern times, one whose imaginative sweep would dwarf the notions of Ford or Nuffield.

I was entranced with the spectacle of the tycoon-to-be and looked forward to being a rich man's son. Father decided to take over a newsagent's shop, a business that apparently could be run profitably by a child. Newspapers, tobacco, cigarettes, snuff, bundles of sticks, firelighters, simple toys, sweets and assorted 'fancy goods'—these were always in demand by the workers in east Belfast. So off we went, our small family of three, to Belfast, city of mercantile dreams. Father had the addresses of several

shops with 'a good passing trade' on main roads. These he
visited and assessed. He chatted with proprietors, asked awkward
questions, scrutinised accounts, considering both tactics and
strategy.

All the chatter and to-and-froing excited me, for I knew that
the trade winds were blowing hard, now that the hedgerows and
potato drills and carts had been left behind. It was hurrah for
each till whose every ring would be the music of thanksgiving, a
salute to Protestant enterprise. Farewell to the little school
where I was an honoured heretic, and goodbye to the sickly
warm stench of Castleblayney market days full of pigs' squeals
and horny-handed cattle-dealers' be-Jasuses—and a sad goodbye
to Victor, wisest of collies.

After much enquiry and reflection—and perhaps even prayer
by mother—father settled for a newspaper shop, on the
Newtownards Road, called the 'Kenilworth'. The good passing
trade was an attraction for him, just as the association with Sir
Walter Scott was an attraction for me. He opened an account
with the Northern Bank at the top of the road, near the
Holywood Arches. We would end up with a store like Robb's or
even Woolworth's in the High Street near the Albert Clock, but
naturally one had to start somewhere.

I was enrolled at the new elementary school in Templemore
Avenue, the biggest building but for the City Hall I had yet seen.
It smelled of fresh paint and wood shavings and disinfectant.
Unfortunately for me, it was solidly Protestant—so there would
be no way of escape from morning assembly. I consoled myself
with the fact that Protestants prayed less than Catholics. O
bustling, rainy city with swings and slides in the children's
playground at Scotch Row (locked up, of course, on Sundays
when all good children were at home studying the Bible or at
Sunday School).

But have I, by any chance, suggested that delights were hard
to come by? Time took care of that. I discovered the solidarity
and the intrigues of the back streets, the politics of children's
leisure time. By politics I mean the little groupings and alliances,

the fallings-out and the fights all based on personal attractions and clashes. Mother gave strict instructions that I could not absent myself without permission given or refused at our business headquarters, the Kenilworth, where we lived over the shop. I often had to ask the question: "Have you the right time, mister?"

Crowds of boys appeared on all sides—new potential friends, new potential enemies. Helpful, cheerful, tidy little boys roamed the streets, as did others who were double-faced, malicious, dirty. Yet they were all of the Protestant tribe. It was considered wrong, even dangerous, to tangle with the Catholic nationalist tribe. We thought of 'us' and 'them'—we were the good guys, they were the bad guys. Every boy jack of these new boys I began to meet was crammed with city lore. How did you straighten out the metal top of a lemonade bottle? Simple—just place it on a tram-line and wait for a tram to pass. How did you see part of a football match? Wait outside until half-time and then walk in. What did the sign 'FP' mean? Father's prick, of course.

Now my own father could hardly be called a bookman, although he did express admiration for Samuel Lover's novel, *Handy Andy*. But, to give him his due, he assiduously combed through the racing pages of the newspapers like a true student of form. From gambling, as from his business venture, he had high hopes of making a fortune. This hope was dashed in the end for, in his own words, his horses "never ran fast enough". The handful of books in our home were all musty Victorian or Edwardian novels that had survived two fires and a number of removals. I remember there was a book entitled *A House Divided*, a good forecast of what our own home would be in the years to come.

Mother liked a 'nice story', but never seemed to have time to settle with a book or magazine. She could never understand why I shied away from writing 'nice stories', nor could she understand why editors would pay to have novels reviewed. This amazed her as much as D.H. Lawrence amazed his father when he showed him a cheque that was an advance on an early novel. The father is supposed to have exclaimed: "Eh, Bert, and to think tha's never done a day's work in thy life!" Father's advice was to write something that would 'take' and that could be done by making people laugh.

He used to nip out to McMahon's pub or the Green Bar for a 'wee drink' more frequently than befitted a respectable merchant hoping to rake in the shekels in an acquisitive society, and in which the ugly spectre of unemployment was never absent. We lived, after all, in the hungry 1930s and the north of Ireland was a depressed area. Our prosperity as shopkeepers depended fairly directly on conditions at the Island, where the ships were built. A cold fear gripped us when we heard that a large number of men had been paid off or that Belfast had lost an order to the Clyde. Didn't everyone know that our ships were the best in the world! We didn't care to dwell on the fate of the 'unsinkable' *Titanic.*

As father became more experienced, he talked less about shops being goldmines. Snags were discovered. Times were hard, money was tight, newsboys unreliable, assistants dishonest and customers owing bills could do a midnight flit to somewhere in the Shankill. There we were, then, surrounded by newspapers, weekly magazines, big jars of brightly-coloured 'boilings' (sweets guaranteed to rot the teeth), packets and packets of cigarettes (guaranteed to make boys into men), mellow-smelling bars of plug tobacco bought by mature citizens and canisters of snuff for the elderly ladies. I was allowed to serve in the shop and I loved it. There seemed an insatiable appetite for our wares—an appetite so tremendous that if the shop were unattended for a few minutes it could mean a theft!

We were proud of the gentle craft of newsagency. Not every Tom, Dick and Harry could set up as a supplier of the *Belfast Telegraph*, the *Northern Whig* and *News Letter* to customers eager for the latest developments in football, horse racing and local politics. I often pored over these pages myself and read of 'Slip-it-to Joe' Bambrick's latest triumph at Windsor Park. I read too of the burning of some building in Berlin called the Reichstag and what a man called Herr Hitler had just said or done. He always seemed in bad temper, whoever he was. Mother said she could not understand why the Germans had fought a war against us. They were Protestants, weren't they? I learned what I could about local politicians—Lord Craigavon, J.M. Andrews, Sir Wilson Hungerford, Tommy Henderson, the Labour leader Harry Midgley. I absorbed information about foreigners too. There was a Herr von Papen who always seemed to be travelling throughout Europe. I often wondered what he was up to. Then there was the man who ruled Italy, Signor Benito Mussolini, but all I knew about Italians was that they made good ice cream. Perhaps Signor Mussolini's father had been one of their notable ice cream merchants. Not least I liked to read about the kings of sport, men like Don Bradman and Kaye Don.

Occasionally, I was sent down—great privilege that it was—to collect our copies of the sixth edition at the *Belfast Telegraph* offices or, as we preferred to call it, Baird's. A sharp-eyed newsboy might catch a glimpse of the legendary figure of Sir Robert Baird. At 'the hole' could be seen a cross-section of Belfast youth who had entered the world of commerce at an early age. These lads seethed with energy. They had ready fists in case of dispute and some were well-equipped with an extensive vocabulary of obscene language. Those not so tough would hurl milder threats at their rivals.

It was after a visit to 'the hole' that I conceived the idea that when I grew up I would not merely sell newspapers, like father, but would—heaven help me!—actually write in them. I had seen films of American newspapermen in shirt sleeves and wearing eyeshades—such a career seemed romantic, though how one went about translating romance into reality I had no idea whatever. I was silly enough to mention my dream to father. His comment was like a blow on the head: "These journalist fellows drink like fish and they usually die in the workhouse." No matter, I thought, that's what I'll be one day—a journalist. Didn't the novelist Dickens start out as a journalist? If he could do it, why couldn't I? He too had had some trouble with his feckless father.

In truth, father's opposition stimulated me as I had come to suspect that his attitude towards me was based less on an objective study of the situation than sheer jealousy. As a child I did not quite see it in that light—I would never have used 'jealousy' in my own mind. But I felt there was something odd about his readiness to throw cold water on my dreams.

Since I have grown up—and especially since his death in 1950—I have frequently relived the various crises in which he and I confronted each other, and which have had so strong an influence on my subsequent emotional life. The father-son relationship, always difficult—sometimes to the point of impossibility—was rather bitter in our case; and it seems likely that father had been driven to repeating with me the pattern he had established with his own father. Another revealing aspect of father's behaviour was his refusal to attend his mother's funeral. Did he feel that he had been unjustly deprived of love? That the other sons had been preferred at his expense? It seems a likely explanation for his having taken to drink as a solution for his problems.

As the years passed, I grew more and more like the other 'wee fellows'. I steered a course between being an ill-mannered roughneck on the one hand and a 'cissy' on the other. I had no great taste for the rough-housing that was practised, but I would not stand for being bullied. I made it a rule to let the other fellow strike the first blow. Then I would hit him back—harder, if I possibly could. It was a philosophy widely understood in east Belfast. Perhaps it is a philosophy that is understood everywhere.

From time to time, I would walk as far as the Queen's Bridge or the Albert Memorial with its enormous clock. On the bridge, I would look eagerly at the ships that voyaged to fabulous places like Liverpool and Glasgow. Among the people I knew, few ventured far except those driven out by poverty and the hope of employment elsewhere. Tourism lay in the distant future.

A one-legged man used to sit on the bridge. It seemed wrong to me as a child that a man should expose his injuries for gain, that he had no one to look after him. Had God punished him for some terrible sin? Had he been the victim of a stroke of ill luck?

Was he just lazy? I did not know the answer. Some boys said that begging was a trade like any other. Beggars did well out of it. I did not know. Life around me had its visible quota of poverty and suffering. Times were hard, as I was constantly reminded. All around I could see ragged, smelly children, some of them suffering from rickets or TB. I could also see shawled, anaemic women, brutal men, cripples and deaf-mutes and the blind, tramps and derelicts. What was the meaning of it all? Perhaps one day I would find out.

It was a world of characters too. Old soldiers, now stiff and peevish, would speak of trench warfare in the 'Big War' and boast of how many Huns they had killed. Or they might go further back in history and talk of their service in South Africa or the Punjab. Then there was the less martial, but certainly not less dignified, personage called Joe, who was in command of the trap which delivered copies of the *Belfast Telegraph*. Vans were in fairly general use even then, but they could not compete in smartness with a trap drawn by a well-groomed horse.

On Sundays, I was packed off to Sunday school and church—as much to get me out of the way as to have me save my immortal soul. Not that being 'saved' had a high place in Presbyterianism. What seemed to matter more was to live an upright life. Moral and religious instruction was pleasant, since there was no fearsome exam to be passed at the end of it. The exam, so to speak, was life itself. Eventually one had to face the Supreme Headmaster and account for what one had done and not done on this earth. Sunday was a shut day for the pubs, so father never drank on the Sabbath—as we sometimes called Sunday—for no strong drink was kept in the house. I think this was not so much a matter of principle but rather because mother had threatened to pour down the sink any alcohol she came across.

Sunday work was deprecated and I used to be reminded that homework done on a Sunday would not prosper, though it seemed to me not a matter of much concern to my schoolmasters. I detected an element of hypocrisy here as in so many other matters. Good Presbyterians only did necessary work on a

Sunday, but how exactly did one define the adjective 'necessary'? Sunday was the day I most enjoyed our mid-day meal, 'dinner' as we called it, which usually consisted of roast beef or boiled beef with the inevitable potatoes and cabbage, followed by jelly and strong tea. On Saturday evening, I delighted in cutting up the large square of thick jelly, pouring boiling water over it and floating slices of banana on top. The Sunday meal could be relished, for not only would father be sober but we could eat unhurriedly. There would be no rushing out to the shop when the bell rang to serve customers, as often happened during the week, and coming back to find on one's plate a tepid, greasy mess.

On Saturdays, I went to the butcher's and picked up a nice joint or piece of boiling beef. I was quite a judge of prices and was encouraged by my thrifty mother to find bargains. Value for money was what I aimed at. While not being poor, like people in the drab side-streets, we still had to count every penny. Nothing that could be used was thrown away. There was much worry about money and this seemed to me to contradict our belief that God would provide. Still, bills had to be paid and mother believed in prompt payment. Father helped himself too readily to the takings, squandering money on drink and betting. We never had the feeling of financial security. My parents' house had in it little affection and laughter, and too much anger and bitterness.

"If a man hasn't made his fortune by the time he's forty," said father, "then he never will." He himself had failed to make the fortune he talked about or, if he had, he had lost it. As I lay in my attic bed and twilight deepened into darkness, and the shrill noise of lads and girls still at play lessened, I pondered this question of a fortune in the candlelight. How much was a fortune? £100? £1,000? £10,000? Rich men, it was well known, wore plus fours, played golf, drank champagne for breakfast and lived in enormous houses. And yet, oddly enough, the Bible did not seem to favour rich men. They had to die just like tramps and the one-legged beggar who sat on the Queen's Bridge. Rumour had it the rich were unhappy. What a puzzling world we lived in! I wished to chat with a wise man who would straighten out my contradictory notions.

At school, I began to hear whispers, and more than whispers, of the strange thing called 'sex'. Some of the bolder and more precocious boys, especially those who had sisters and brothers older than themselves, began to speak of secret practices and delights. Willie Taggart had tales to tell of what he had actually seen with his own eyes in dark entries or deserted quarries. His stories were corroborated by other boys, some of whom I had actually seen exposing their genitals to tittering girls. The general belief was that sex was both disgusting and delightful. If it was disgusting, why did people indulge in it? I was genuinely puzzled, but the matter remained mysterious. Not one of the adults I knew could be questioned on such a topic.

Willie Taggart had an Answer Book in which could be found the solutions to arithmetic problems. I got into the habit of going to his house after school and copying down the answers. Then I knew how many sums I had got right before spotty Mr. Ferguson examined my work. (I always aimed at getting three or at most four right out of five. Five out of five would look suspicious.) In the security of his home, where I never met either of his parents, Willie played the genial host and undertook further lessons in my sexual education. Sometimes I emerged rather shamefaced. I at last stopped quarrelling with his facts, for he showed me diagrams in a well-thumbed book to back up his assertions. But I refused to believe that the sort of people we knew did the things Willie said they did. Willie Taggart affronted me by saying that even clergymen did these things.

"Why do they preach against sex, then?" I asked him.

"That is simple," Willie replied. "They're all hypocrites. That's what me da says."

When I went home and thought over what Willie had told me, I found my belief in the purity of clergymen somewhat weakened. Teachers, too, I wondered, and doctors and perhaps my own parents? It did not bear thinking about. Then I reflected that

Willie had known how to get hold of an Answer Book. He had actually ventured into some posh bookshop—I had never set foot in such a place—and bought it with his pocket money. Had I entered a bookshop, I imagined I would be confronted by a grim, bald gent (a BA no doubt) who would have asked gruffly: "And why might you want an Answer Book, young man?"

Why, he might even have called a policeman and then I would have been in real trouble. Such a picture of events would not have occurred to the matter-of-fact Willie. Willie knew how things were done in the world. He knew that, if you had the money in your hand, you could buy almost anything. He was a realist, I a romantic.

Though sex seemed disgusting, I used to daydream of marrying a beautiful girl when I grew up, someone who looked like a princess. She would have long blonde hair and speak like one of those ladies I heard on the wireless, and I would be heroic and famous, perhaps having rescued her from drowning. Some of the local girls were pretty, though they were far from being princesses, as I discovered in the case of Mary Anderson. When Mary came into the shop I always gave her a few extra sweets. Evidently she told her friends, for they began to think I had cheated them. My interest in Mary ended abruptly when I heard her make a coarse remark. Girls then were not exclusively made of sugar and spice, but had other aspects too. Willie Taggart could have informed me about girls.

One day I woke up with a really nasty cold. The day after that I was even worse. I was in great discomfort, for my nose and throat were sore and inflamed. I could not eat. At the hospital in Templemore Avenue, they discovered, by means of a swab, that I had diphtheria. Next came the ambulance and a drive through the streets out to Purdysburn Fever Hospital where I found myself in a ward full of subdued children and cheerful nurses. I remember having injections in the thigh and wondering whether I would live. Would my sins be forgiven?

Soon the cloud lifted. I grew stronger and was transferred to a convalescent ward where I luxuriated in the company of a

30

swarm of noisy extroverts. Father came laden with bananas and sympathy and wearing his nattiest blue serge suit. I felt proud of him. Why could he not always be like that? I enjoyed my status as the Boy Who Had Nearly Died. When I went home, the house smelled fresh. It had been fumigated and then repainted.

Soon after my return, mother opened a letter with a Free State stamp on the envelope. It was from Aunt Liz-Ann down in Co. Monaghan. She would be delighted to have me there, the country air and fresh eggs and cream and butter and home-cured bacon would soon have me as right as rain. I could stay at least a month. A month in the country! No school, fields to roam at will, droll Uncle George with his tall stories, the collie dog to play with, the wild cats to chase ... a dream world was opening up for me.

Mother hesitated. She was afraid I might not be able to get there by myself and there was nobody to accompany me. But I set her mind at rest. Yes, of course I could travel to Castleblayney on my own ... I was a big boy now, nearly twelve ... yes of course I would get into the right train when I changed at Dundalk. I could read! I could ask! Uncle George would be at Castleblayney Station with his mare, Bessie, to meet me. Nothing has ever been so delightful both in anticipation—and in the event.

On the day of my leaving for the Great Northern Station, I was a-tingle with excitement. My shiny brown suitcase had been crammed with socks and shirts, and patched old trousers for country wear, and I was shod in a pair of gleaming black boots that would soon be muddied in the country fields and lanes. I went up to the butcher's for a pound of pork sausages for mother intended to send me off with a full stomach. I ran into Willie who was mitching that day. I told him where I was going. He was incredulous.

"But that's in the Free State," he exclaimed. "You'll be murdered there."

"No, I won't," I said. "I lived there for a while once and went to a village school where I was the only Protestant."

"Didn't the Fenians beat you up?" asked Willie.

31

"No, they didn't. I got friendly with a Catholic boy called Sean. I'll be seeing him soon."

Willie was astonished.

He changed the subject. He sniggered and whispered confidentially: "Now when you're in the country take a keek at them bulls an' cows. I saw what they were up to once."

Willie was a practical lad, a wise urchin of the back streets, cunning and canny yet loyal to his friends. There was so much he knew that I didn't. Yet I had the feeling that perhaps I knew a thing or two undreamed of in Willie Taggart's philosophy,

Willie would not understand that, in the shadowy fields where dusk would find me, there were banks "on which the wild thyme blows/Where oxlips and the nodding violet grows". That was what I had read and remembered from some book at school. It sounded lovely, though I knew poetry had no practical value except perhaps in exams. I did not know what 'thyme' was and was not sure of the pronunciation. The country sights were before me as I stood clutching my brown-paper parcel of pork sausages, and the scent of the country was already in my nostrils. In a few hours time, the hills and lakes of Co. Monaghan would be as real as Fraser Street, where I said goodbye to Willie Taggart.

THREE

The Sash My Father Wore

I shuttled between two houses: the house-*cum*-shop my Aunts Tillie and Annie ran in Broadway, and the Kenilworth, my parents' house-*cum*-shop in the Newtownards Road. From west Belfast to east Belfast, only a few miles apart—but, for a child, the North and South Poles. Sometimes, I would stay for long, idyllic periods—months in duration—with my aunts, week-ending reluctantly with my parents, in tears when at last I boarded the red tram taking me to the Junction, where I got on another red tram which would cross the Queen's Bridge into territory for which I had no liking.

There was a time when I must have spent up to three years with my parents, only occasionally visiting Broadway and going on the annual jaunt to Co. Monaghan, where I often stayed as long as six weeks with father's sister. This was the Belfast period when I was a pupil at the huge, glassy, shining school in Templemore Avenue. I endured, rather than enjoyed, that school though it had its satisfactions—such as my friendship with Willie Taggart, Dickie Best and Fat Mayne. I had my second fight on the way home from school (the first fight, a less serious affair, was at a Cub meeting when the other lad bled my nose). Fortunately, I put up a reasonable show so that I did not shame my friends. Cowardice might even have left me friendless. It was the willingness to fight that counted, not the winning.

33

I loathed my parents' house as much as I loved my aunts'. In one there was dissension and quarrelling, in the other cheerfulness and good humour. My aunts believed in God and prayer, and they made a success of their business. Mother did not seem to have much imagination, but had the virtues of hard work and patience with which to withstand the moods and inadequacies of father. His dreams of business success had crumbled. During the boom of the First World War, he had done well, exporting eggs and butter to a hungry England. Those were the days when England's difficulty had been Ireland's opportunity. What did the slaughter in France matter, so long as hard-faced men could make money? Not, indeed, that father was hard-faced. He was simply weak.

I often wondered what he had looked like as a young man. It seemed to me that, with his dark, glossy hair and faintly Spanish appearance, he must have been attractive. Mother no doubt had believed what he told her about his future prospects, though her mother and sisters had disapproved of him. She was big-boned and fair, and I resembled her.

Mother was meek and conformist, which I was not. Boys at the elementary school had told me that fighting back accomplishes more than giving in to the other fellow. Yet Christ, I had been told, said one should not hit back. Willie Taggart's philosophy was one of cheerful aggression and of taking small, calculated risks. All this confused me. Yet it seemed pretty clear that people, especially adults, did not practise what they preached. Catholics and republicans were our enemies, weren't they? Jesus said we should love our enemies and there was general agreement we should follow the Master. Did we love our enemies? We did not.

'Ven' was the name which my mother and her two sisters used when they met in a coven and talked about my father. They could safely use it when the old boy was within hearing distance. He never cottoned on, and thought perhaps they were gossiping about someone they had known in the old days in Derry. Ven was an abbreviation for Venezuela, and they sometimes giggled as they spoke the longer form. This nickname seemed to cause them infinite amusement. It helped them to overcome their contempt for somebody they considered a drunken failure. I never did find out why they had chosen this particular nickname. Perhaps he had once read out a news item or something of the kind from the 'Tally'—as everyone called the evening paper, the *Belfast Telegraph*—that had to do with the South American republic. Children sometimes ask a lot of questions. But about some matters they wisely keep quiet, believing that acceptance is best. They know that grown-ups will not answer certain questions truthfully. I never heard the old man refer to Venezuela or South America, for his terms of reference were strictly local. He had never been further away from base than London and I remember him telling me about a big railway station there called Houston or so I imagined him to say. Perhaps he unconsciously picked up a cockney porter's rendering of Euston.

I tried to please him but found I could not, so in the end I gave up trying. As I grew older, we had more and more disputes. He had a violent, uncontrollable temper. He often frightened me and I feared for my life as for my mother's. In a drunken rage, he would throw his dinner into the fire, and, on one occasion, I remember he pulled an electric light fitting out of the wall in the kitchen so that the wires dangled obscenely. Violence seemed something that men indulged in—or some men at least, for I had never seen my uncles behave in such a way.

But it would be wrong to suppose that father and I were always at enmity. Sometimes, when he was in a good mood, I would sit on his knee and comb the dark hair that was beginning to silver at the sides. Or we would go out together on placid, golden-tinted summer evenings, sauntering up the drab Short Strand and onwards to the leafy oasis of Ormeau Park, where decades earlier the young Forrest Reid used to listen to the strains of a German band. Mother talked about these German bands that had been a feature of Ulster life before the First World War. The only foreigners in Belfast in my time were a handful of Italians, who ran ice cream shops and sold fish and chips. Nobody I knew would have touched *pasta*.

I had a football which I obtained by saving up a set of football cards (each card represented a team and could be found in copies of boys' papers such as *The Wizard* and *The Rover*). As a newsagent's son, I was in a favoured position so, in the end, I completed the set. I posted it off to the publishers in London and got my football. Dad and I would find a secluded place in the Ormeau Park where we could kick it around for fun, free from the deadly competitiveness of boys for whom football was a religion. He would advise me on such excursions to work hard at school so that I would be a credit to the family. Yet he had some reservations about 'the family'. I sensed a bitterness in him for— referring to the family, his brothers and sister—he would say: "Get yourself a good job and then you can snap your fingers at the whole lot of them."

Perhaps he had been dependent on their help and resented being patronised. I was too young to understand and, in later years, have regretted that I never came to understand his viewpoint and the cause of his being the black sheep.

We would begin our journey home, ball safely tucked under oxter. The way back would then turn into a roll-call of pubs— Kelly's, Murphy's, the Marble Bar, the City Lights, the Britannia. I would wait outside each one and listen to the sea-noise of babble within. I would walk up and down, bounce the ball on the pavement, and wince as groups of rough lads went past spitting out side-of-the-mouth jeers at the too-respectable-looking boy with a football—"Did ya knuck it from the Athletic Stores, you?" Out father would come at last, flecks of sawdust on his laced-up boots and we would soldier on through the now lighted streets.

After every stop for refreshment, he would be that bit less sure-footed. Near the end of the journey, his earlier good humour would have disappeared. He would grasp me by the arm and mutter incoherently that mother's family had robbed him and that he would have a writ served on them and get every penny piece back. My cheeks damp with tears and my heart bursting with shame, the pair of us would shuffle back to the Kenilworth to hear mother's lamentations: "I might have known it." Needless to say, it did not always end so badly, and my hopes of a pleasant outcome were not always frustrated. Yet I tend to recall the occasions when a drunk father would unlace his boots and kick them off in the kitchen before crawling upstairs to bed. I learnt the hard way about the abuse of alcohol.

Father had few friends for he preferred to drink alone, and to go from pub to pub rather than have a local. But for a time he had indeed one friend, a merry-eyed, cuddly little man called Alfie Duggan. Alfie bubbled over with cheer and chatter. His words frothed out of him and he laughed, so mother said, 'fit to beat the band'. Alfie was employed as a canvasser for the *Daily Herald*, a newspaper that offered free gifts in return for taking the paper for a specified period. These gifts were sets of Dickens or encyclopaedias that most working-class people would open a few times and then set aside for ever, but which their wives would dust with that Protestant zeal for cleanliness that, I learned at Sunday school, is next to godliness. With his sense of fun Alfie proved a success as a canvasser. Many would do anything if they were 'codded' into it, including buying newspapers they did not want so as to get free gifts they did not want.

The bond between father and Alfie was membership of the same Orange lodge, Loyal Orange Lodge No. 525, a number that pleased me because it read the same from right to left as from left to right. Father's joyless, anxious temperament was drawn to Alfie's fizzy extroversion. Mother approved of father's membership of the Order. Was it not right and proper that a man should uphold his religious principles in the face of Catholic wiliness and Fenian treachery? Just look at the face of that half-Spaniard de Valera and note the trickiness written all over it! You couldn't trust one of them.

Yet mother had to admit that some Catholics were good people and some Protestants bad people. I found all this talk puzzling. I liked black-and-white situations. Then there was the fact that being an Orangeman in east Belfast was good for business. Even Catholics—and some were customers whom we served with courtesy and efficiency—respected a man who stood

37

firm on fundamental issues. There was no clash between devotion to the Crown and the half-crown. God, it was widely understood, favoured those who helped themselves. He favoured Presbyterians in particular. Another puzzle for me lay in a phrase in one of our prayers: 'the holy Catholic church'. I assumed that the printer was either no theologian or else a Catholic who cunningly inserted it as propaganda for Rome.

It was odd that our great folk hero was a Dutchman, William III—no Presbyterian, surely? Then there were the more recent, local heroes like the histrionic southerner Lord Carson, or Sir Edward Carson as older people called him, and the granite-faced Sir James Craig who had been elevated to Lord Craigavon. Mother had her doubts about Craigavon, as she believed he had made money out of whiskey. Of all our folk festivals, the crowning one took place on July 12th and it, as every schoolboy knew, celebrated the Battle of the Boyne in 1690 when William of Orange defeated the forces of the Catholic James II.

We had all heard of the historic toast that runs: "To the glorious, pious and immortal memory of King William III, who saved us from rogues and roguery, slaves and slavery, knaves and knavery, Popes and Popery, from brass money and wooden shoes ..." Another great festival was the August 12th celebration in Derry, or Londonderry, when the Apprentice Boys, an organisation separate from but parallel to the Orange Order, took to the streets and vowed never to be subject to rule from Dublin or Rome. Mother and my aunts, with their Derry background, believed the Apprentice Boys to be the truest defenders of our faith and way of life.

I did not learn the Protestant version of history from books, but by word of mouth passed on from generation to generation. The 'quality', who had education and leisure, knew the details and the dates, but ordinary folk like ourselves carried the facts—or alleged facts—of history in our very bones and in our hearts. We were the people who had never surrendered and would never surrender. As each Twelfth of July came round, Protestant fervour would rise again and be reaffirmed.

In Sandy Row and the Shankill and the Newtownards Road, street would vie with street in putting up decorative arches tricked out with the symbols we knew and loved: the open Bible, William crossing the Boyne on his white horse, a black servant kneeling at the feet of his sovereign lady, Queen Victoria. Even the name Victoria—Victory—had a triumphalist tone. Crude but emotive paintings of scenes from history would appear on gables in working-class streets. So would slogans such as 'No Surrender', 'Remember 1690' and 'Ulster is not for sale'.

Coming up to the Twelfth, father and Alfie used to show some signs of excitement. Lodge No. 525 must be one of the smartest in the five-mile walk to Finaghy—'the walk' was the term used, presumably to show it was civilian in nature—where speeches would be made and all the old slogans repeated. Finaghy was known as 'the field' and sympathisers who were not themselves Orangemen would also go there. Orangemen tended to wear an unofficial uniform, a blue serge suit and a bowler hat. These Sunday suits needed to be pressed and ironed and made ready for the great day. Alfie would call at the shop and chaff us all, including the customers, and tell a joke or two before he and father sallied out to McMahon's Select Bar for a half-un of Bushmills ('a wee Bush') whiskey and a pint of Guinness or black-and-tan.

"Me and Harry's goin' for a wee drop o' holy water," he would say apologetically to mother, knowing that she disapproved.

One story Alfie told with glee was about a visiting Englishman—and strangely enough the abstraction 'England' was loved but the English were treated with some reserve—who watched a Twelfth of July procession with its banners tossing in the wind and its brawny men flagellating Lambeg drums until the drummer's wrists ran with blood, and its flute and pipe bands accompanying the marchers, and its ranks of be-sashed, determined Ulstermen who had summoned up all their martial qualities for the occasion. Well, this Englishman watched the tribal display and was impressed by its ferocious dedication, but being an Englishman, and by definition ignorant of even the

39

basic facts of Irish—or indeed *any*—history, could make nothing whatever of it. He turned to a bystander and said in his BBC-ish voice: "Could you please tell me what these good people are celebrating?" The bystander, scandalised by both the display of ignorance and the English upper-class accent, retorted more in sorrow than in anger: "Away home, maun, an' read yer Bible."

On the eve of the Twelfth, bonfires were lit and for weeks beforehand children went round shops and houses scrounging wooden boxes and anything that burned readily. These bonfires—pronounced 'bone-fires'—were held in districts where arches and red, white and blue bunting had already been put up. Some said the biggest bonfire of all was in Sandy Row. Others swore by the Shankill and some voices—of which mine was one—were raised on behalf of the Newtownards Road, a district where, in late June and early July, men would be busy painting their houses, frequently—so it was said—with paint purloined from Harland & Wolff's shipyard.

Catholics were reputed to stay behind locked doors on the evening of July 11th, except for those among them spoiling for a fight with the Billy Boys. In my time, such fights might result in some injury but not in death as had happened in the past and was to happen in the future. I was a devotee of bonfires, not so much for their political or religious significance as for their friendly pagan warmth. The crackle and the flames inflamed excitement, and gave some of us Prods a deep sense of belonging. God's Chosen People—not the Jews, but ourselves—would leap and skip and caper round the blaze and, when the great fire had been reduced to a few smoking embers, we would creep sadly away to snatch a few hours' sleep before the start of the truly serious business of the following day.

It was on a drizzling Twelfth of July in the early 1930s that I stood on the Newtownards Road and watched the Ballymacarret and East Belfast Orange contingents marching—walking?— towards the central meeting point from which the assembled lodges of the Belfast area would move towards Finaghy. There they would picnic, drink beer (except for the minority of rabid teetotallers), eat ice cream and listen to the thunder of the orators. I watched eagerly for a glimpse of father and Alfie, those pillars of Ulster-is-Right-and-Ulster-will-Fight philosophy. My guarder-of-Derry's-walls father walked in the over-sober, rather stiff way affected by heavy drinkers who, for once, must rely on their own will and nerve. He wore the regulation blue suit with a snowy white handkerchief peeping out of the breast pocket, and a bowler hat he had borrowed from Mr. Hanna, the proprietor of the near-by hardware shop. Alfie half-danced along at father's side, grinning and waving to acquaintances in the crowd who would wave back. He looked too jovial a man to be a descendant of the stern Scottish settlers of the 16th century. I began to suspect that wee Alfie had a drop of foreign blood in him.

The crowd roared in delight as the flute band played the stirring song that has carried many a Protestant into battle, not least some of the soldiers of the Ulster Division who died on the Somme—'The Sash My Father Wore'. Bystanders waved Union Jacks with abandon and joined in the words of the old Orange classic:

It's old but it is beautiful,
Its colours they are fine,
It was worn at Derry, Aughrim,
Enniskillen and the Boyne.
My father wore it when a youth
In bygone days of yore,
So on the Twelfth I proudly wear
The sash my father wore.

My mind turned to the sash my father was wearing. It was kept in a metal box in the coal-hole and the moth balls had preserved it from all harm. Once a year, the old, frayed sash was taken out with due reverence. One day, I thought, I will be wearing it.

The procession moved on. I had watched father and Alfie and their fellow lodge members go by with pride, but also with a

41

sense of bitter disappointment. As well as the two stalwart Orangemen supporting each banner, there were also a couple of lads who held the strings that kept the banner in position, especially on a windy day. I had wanted to hold a string and begged father to ask the Master of his Lodge if I might have that honour. Father said yes, he would, but he reckoned without Aunt Tillie.

"It looks as if I'm going to hold a string on the Twelfth," I told her artlessly.

"You'll do no such daft thing," Aunt Tillie replied.

"But father says I can—I mean, if the Master of the Lodge agrees," I insisted.

"I don't care what your father says or what the Master of the Lodge says or what Lord Craigavon himself says, you will not go traipsing through the streets of Belfast on the Twelfth or you'll know the reason why," said Aunt Tillie firmly.

Now when Aunt Tillie made up her mind she really meant what she said. I could defy father or disobey mother, but I could not oppose Aunt Tillie on an important issue. I knew that of them all she loved me most. I would have to obey.

"But why shouldn't I?" I demanded, for I never gave in without a fight. "Willie Taggart's doing it and so is Tommy Patterson. Why not me?"

"Because," she said, "you are not Willie Taggart or Tommy Patterson. They will leave school at fourteen and go to work in the shipyard or as a message boy for a grocer. I want to see you become somebody, a Presbyterian minister or a doctor. I'm as loyal as the next, but you can put the notion of walking through the streets right out of your head."

It was noteworthy that, except for the teetotallers among the Orangemen, the homeward procession was more joyous and relaxed than the journey out to the field. The movements of the banner-bearers were more balletic, less stiff. Their joints had been oiled by John Barleycorn. Father and Alfie were not counted among the teetotallers, so they came back clutching each other for support.

"Hi, you two, are youse married?" cried a wit among the onlookers.

Alfred lunged out ineffectively and cried, "Get out of the road, ye Fenian bugger!"

And so another Twelfth of July ended with more whimper than bang. But there would be another and another and another, so long as the Protestant enclave existed in Ireland's north. Once again the patriarchs of the Order would sit like graven images in horse-drawn landaus and the men in blue serge and bowlers would step out briskly to the music, sometimes merry, sometimes provocative. Occasionally, there would be an eruption of violence when fists and stones would fly. Worse still, there might be a crackle of gunfire. Or the sky at evening would redden from a blaze that signalled the burning of a Catholic house in a Protestant area or a Protestant house in a Catholic area. Our side was naturally always in the right. We never started trouble. 'They' did.

The watered-silk sash father had worn so proudly was wrapped up in tissue paper along with the moth balls and placed reverently in the tin box. Sometimes it was taken out and shown to a tipsy companion as proof of father's commitment to King Billy's cause. But, as the years passed and the creditors pressed for payment, father lost interest. He stopped going to Lodge meetings and even lost touch with Loyal Orange Lodge No. 525. The business gradually declined. Competition was strong. Mother could not cope with all the work on her own. Father drank more and more heavily, and took less and less responsibility.

In the end, the Kenilworth was sold up and my parents went their separate ways. And the sash? What happened to it? It would be pleasing to think that father took it with him in the tin box to his lodgings, but I have no reason to think that he did. Was it left behind in the coal-hole? Did he pawn it for the price of a few whiskeys? Now that father is dead, I shall never know. Yet I sometimes wonder where it got to—and, when I do, I see father and little Alfie stepping out to the brave music. The sacred Orange words come into mind:

43

My father wore it when a youth
In bygone days of yore,
So on the Twelfth I proudly wear
The sash my father wore.

FOUR

The Streets of Freedom

"Now I don't want you to play with these rough wee fellows," said mother. She went on: "The chemist across the road, Mr. Quirke, has three of the nicest boys you would find anywhere. Why don't you play with them?"

In the Kenilworth, we sold the local and English newspapers, bar tobacco, cigarettes, snuff, lemonade and a strange drink called Sarsaparilla, chocolate, boiled sweets, firelighters, bundles of sticks and balls of string, to mention a few items at random. I helped myself to sweets and lemonade fairly generously, though within limits set by mother who warned me "not to eat the profits".

We belonged to the class of small but respectable shopkeepers whose function had not been usurped by the large combines, although that process had already started. People of our sort hated, really *hated*, the Co-operative Society, and had a distaste for the chain shops that could under-cut us. We believed in a sort of one-man-one-shop economy. Nor did we subscribe to the philosophy that all men were equal. We felt superior to manual and skilled workers—after all, we were small-scale capitalists.

Yet being your own master, though it sounded marvellous, meant that you were everybody's servant. It meant being pleasant to people you might detest. It meant longer hours of work than if you were an employee protected by a trade union. Even so, we

45

took a great pride in deluding ourselves that we could do as we pleased.

Mother had had a hard life, having been one of a family of four children when her mother was left a widow with next to no financial resources. How my grandmother managed to bring up her children I never discovered. Mother, like her two sisters, wanted life to be easier and more secure for me. How better, then, than to have me cultivate the children of a professional man—"Mr. Quirke is almost a doctor, you know"—and keep clear of the riff-raff who lived in tiny kitchen houses and shamelessly hung out their washing?

On mother's prompting, I approached the eldest of the Quirke children, a boy named John who was approximately my own age. This John turned out to be thin and chalky-faced, as if he lived his life in a basement where they grew mushrooms. He was too polite and, worst of all, he lisped. I knew that, despite his father being "almost a doctor" and John's having won Sunday School prizes, he would never be a friend of mine.

I yearned for the streets of freedom in which the scruffy children played late and early in their torn jerseys. They shinned up walls, they got their knees cut, they tormented cats, they teased shop assistants, they used bad language, they formed themselves into gangs that fought other gangs, they went off with jam jars and nets to catch spricks and some rose to heights I did not aspire to, like breaking windows and shoplifting. These were my heroes and I wanted to be accepted by them. Live dangerously—well, in moderation, for I had a sneaking feeling I was too conformist by half.

Now, Willie Jeffers was a hero. He knew how to get into the cinema and football grounds without payment. He rode free inside tramcars or clung outside, to the annoyance of conductors who tried to beat him off, but feared he might be killed when the tram was in motion. Willie knew where to find conkers and luscious blackberries. He terrorised rivals, but led a band of disreputable friends. If he was sent to a reformatory he said he knew how to escape, not that he was ever put the test. Willie had a strong contempt for girls and the games they played, their skipping and 'shop' and mother-and-child.

Street-wise lads like Willie were football mad, not that any of them owned a leather ball. At a pinch, a tin can would serve and goal posts could be outlined with a piece of chalk some enterprising boy had filched from his classroom. If anyone actually wanted to play proper football, then he and his pals would leave the streets and find a piece of waste ground where they could play, undisturbed by silly girls and envious boys not asked to join in.

Next to football came go-car racing. These vehicles were made out of old soap boxes fitted out with small wheels, and a piece of string for steering. A boy pushed until the contrivance went at such speed that he could no longer keep up with it. There used to be races round the streets—and heaven help the pedestrian who got in the way of a competitor. Respect for person or property was not part of the creed of these youthful aces, who dreamed of one day taking part in the Ulster Tourist Trophy race that brought great racing motorists to our province.

Bicycle racing was another pastime and outlet for the competitive instinct. The only prize for winners was the knowledge that he was a champ. Everybody seemed to be graded according to ability. It was just like school, only that the values were different.

Billy Wilson was a champ at marbles, Jimmy Hanna was the acknowledged wizard in soapbox racing, Alec Dunn was an artist with anything round and bounceable. There existed a hierarchy of ability and achievement. A useful pair of fists got a boy quick acceptance into whatever group he fancied, for fights were a common occurrence.

These fights did not last long and seldom left an aftertaste of bitterness. Fair play predominated. There was often a kind of affectionate fighting between us, the teasing playfulness of energetic young animals. Sometimes we heard tell of real, big-scale battles and for us, in our polarised society of rampant sectarianism, these meant clashes between rival gangs of

47

Protestants and Catholics. Encounters took place in which the principal weapons were stones and real injuries could be inflicted, but I was fortunate never to witness any such battle. Exaggeration was not unknown and sometimes, after a squabble, a boy would limp away, tenderly caressing some part of his body as if he were an old sweat back from the trenches. But boys are shrewd and we always knew if someone had suffered a real injury. Then we gave quick aid to friend or enemy.

Playing 'May Queens' was popular with girls, who dressed up their queen in clothes resembling wedding dresses. They would dance her along the streets with a shrill vocal accompaniment. Groups of children and teenagers in high-heeled shoes and old lace curtains would escort their queen and one girl would collect money in an old tin can. If they met a rival queen with her attendants, the air would be filled with angry cries. Part of the May Queen song went something like this:

Our Queen up the river
with your yah-yah-yah
Your Queen down the river
with your yah-yah-yah
Our Queen up the river
And we'll keep her there for ever
with your yah-yah-yah-yah.

At Hallowe'en, we used to wear false faces and try to frighten old ladies. Our toy guns would emit loud bangs and we would let off rockets and catherine wheels, and hold sparklers in our hands. If we had collected enough empty boxes from shops, we would then start a bonfire. Toffee apples on sticks would make their appearance in shops and I think these usually sold for a halfpenny each.

Some amusements were more passive. Film-going meant attendance at the special children's matinee held on Saturday afternoons at the Pop—the Popular Cinema being its grand title—where admission was one penny or, as we said, 'a wing'.

Did I say passive entertainment? Hardly so, for the child audience loudly cheered its heroes and equally loudly hissed its villains. We stood up and shouted our approval or disapproval. Cowboys and rustlers appeared more real to us than our next-door neighbours.

Football matches we looked on as religious rites, but few lads could afford the entrance money to watch the gladiatorial contests between teams such as Linfield and Glentoran. My own loyalty was divided between those two teams, since my aunts lived in the Linfield supporters' area and my parents in a solid Glentoran district. One learnt that it was possible to get in free at half-time when, if the match had been half-hearted, some men would come out muttering darkly about the decline in football standards and obviously heading for the nearest pub to drown their disappointment in a half-un of Bushmills.

One of the great local footballers was Joe Bambrick and a favourite catchphrase of boys playing in the streets would be 'Slip it to Joe'. The giants of the football field such as Bambrick and Elisha Scott were revered by us all. It came as no surprise to me that, many years later, Belfast should produce a footballer of world stature in George Best.

The days I am talking about were spent at the elementary school in Templemore Avenue, a school that seemed to me an immense building with a fantastic acreage of glass. Social contacts came mainly through school and church, the church in question being Westbourne. But I had another way of making acquaintance with those around me. Whenever I could evade mother's vigilant eye, I would make a sortie at evening into the streets—Austin Street, Kenilworth Street, Fraser Street, Wolff Street, Harcourt Street. These for me were the streets of freedom. In them I could be myself, far removed from the do-gooding adults who ran activities such as the Cubs.

My parents employed a couple of part-time lads to deliver newspapers. I helped sometimes and did a little round every Sunday morning before going off to Sunday school. At Christmas, I used to get presents from some of our customers who appreciated my skill in pushing the *People* or the *Sunday Express* so expertly through their letter-boxes.

One boy we employed was called James Haig Mackie, the 'Haig' having been given him at baptism in honour of the First World War general. "Haig," said mother, "is as honest as the day, not like some of them who would steal the eyes out of your head." Yes, Haig was upright, hard-working, well-mannered and destined for higher things than the delivery of newspapers. The odour of tobacco had not polluted Haig's lips. Nor had he ever tasted strong drink, nor had he ever entered a betting shop. I had entered a betting shop when father sent me to put on bets for him—I have the impression that such places were, strictly speaking, illegal, but the police simply turned a blind eye. Haig's secret was that he was, as the Belfast phrase had it, 'good living'. He had been saved.

Haig attended the Elim Tabernacle Church, whose great figure in distant England was called Principal George Jeffreys. On one of Principal Jeffreys' visits to Belfast, that city of a thousand sects, Haig got me to attend a meeting for healing and salvation. As the proceedings went on, I contrasted the emotional atmosphere with that of the Presbyterian church. I was half-attracted and half-sickened by it. Some people went up to the front to be saved. I wavered but, in the end, I decided to stay in my place. So I missed my opportunity which no doubt would have opened up a new way of life for me. Back I went to my double life—pretending to be conformist yet, all the while, seething with revolt and, at every opportunity, seeking out the boys mother had warned me against. Haig became a pastor of the Elim Tabernacle. I preferred, for the time being at least, to roam around the streets of freedom.

FIVE.

Once Upon a Christmas

I looked out through the kitchen window at the drizzle. Would it snow? It always snowed at Christmas in times past, I thought, for snow, crisp and white and even, appeared in most of the Christmas card scenes. "It's been a tiring day," said mother, "not that there's much money to show for it." I was used to hearing it said that times were bad, money was tight and so on. But my mind was on a higher thing than paying the bills. Snow.

I thought of the gentle way snowflakes would fall on the hills ringing the city, on Divis and Cave Hill. Snow in all its virgin purity I would imagine floating down to whiten the rooftops. Not least I could see snow gradually cap the dome of the City Hall and cling to the statues of those Victorian worthies that stood in their frock coats around the huge edifice. Like them, time itself would stand still in an Arctic world.

"Is it going to snow?" I asked.

"It isn't cold enough, thank goodness," mother answered. "Och, it makes such a mess when people tramp through it."

Mother moved over to the fire and warmed her hands over it. They were red and blotched as she suffered badly from chilblains.

"He's away to the usual place," she said. I knew this meant McMahon's pub. I had often peeped in through the frosted glass windows at the dim interior where working men in cloth caps drank their pints of Guinness and the occasional half-un of malt, and talked, sometimes with passion, of horses and football. I should say *gambling* on horse racing, for the average Belfast worker had nothing do with the horses that were rapidly disappearing from the streets.

Hands warmed, she went back to the shop, for the furious jangling of the bell announced a new customer. I took some greasy dishes into the scullery and placed them in the discoloured sink. Then I lifted a food-stained newspaper off the table and replaced it with a clean inside sheet of the *Belfast Telegraph*. We saved tablecloths, pure linen ones, for rare occasions like Christmas Day dinner or when visitors turned up. Then I went out to the shop where mother was cutting bar tobacco.

"Can I help?" I asked.

"Yes," mother answered, "you could weigh out half-an-ounce of snuff for Mrs. Gill."

I did the job with exaggerated precision, standing well away from the dull brown powder so as not to get any in my nostrils and start sneezing. I imagined I was a famous scientist, someone like that Lavoisier I'd heard about at school, conducting an experiment.

It was past ten in the evening when father returned. The pubs closed at ten. The shop had just been closed, and mother and I were sitting by the fire drinking tea. Father brought a man with him called Mr. Ansell who also frequented McMahon's. Mr. Ansell had a great roll of fat at the back of his neck, his belly bulged out like a Lambeg drum and he wore wide, dark-grey trousers. Mr. Ansell contrasted with lean, dark father in his shiny, navy blue serge.

"So you're back," mother said. "You might have come earlier and given me a hand."

"Oh, but I had a wee bit of business to see to. I knew what I was doing, don't you fret, woman. Many's the bit of business is done over a wee drink."

Father winked at Mr. Ansell, who winked in return. They silently congratulated themselves on being members of a man's world.

Mother shook her head unbelieving. "Good evening to you," she said unenthusiastically to Mr. Ansell.

"Good evening ma'm," said Mr. Ansell, with slight flattery in his voice. "I hope I am not intruding."

Within minutes, father had ordered me cheerily to get out the dartboard. I was delighted. Mr. Ansell's jaws trembled like jellies as he stood a trifle unsteadily and aimed at the board. I noticed how bloodshot father's eyes were and how his voice came more country-slow and slurred than when he was sober. It reminded me of those voices just across the border—still Ulster in quality, but with the merest hint of southern intonation. Mother disappeared to get tea for the two men, and the clink of cups and saucers added a treble to the bass of the men's half-drunken cries. Soon dart-playing was over and they were sucking tea noisily out of saucers under mother's disapproving eye. I remembered that she used to say: "Even if you live in a pig-sty, you don't have to behave like a pig."

"A sup of tea," said father, "is hard to beat."

"Ay, it is that," agreed Mr. Ansell.

"Especially when a body's tired after a hard day's work," said mother quietly, but the irony was lost on the tea-drinkers who had started to cope awkwardly with wedges of plum cake.

When there was nothing more to eat or drink, father called for a song. He got up from his swivel-chair and placed a gaunt wooden chair in the centre of the kitchen.

"Now, wee Robbie," he announced, "will entertain our gallant fighting man, Corporal Ansell, who by rights ought to be a Sergeant Major. But sure there's no justice in this life."

Mr. Ansell grinned toothily. Eager to demonstrate my lung-power and win an audience, I stood to attention on the chair and launched into 'Danny Boy', a song I attacked with more gusto than finesse. "It would make you cry," said father, meaning, I hope, that the song was moving, not that my performance was pitiable. "There's nothing like the old Irish songs," father added. "Now give us 'The Minstrel Boy'."

I sang as if the minstrel boy's wild harp had been slung behind me and Mr. Ansell made noises of approval. I ended up with reciting Kipling's 'If', a poem whose moral uplift made it a popular piece in the puritan north.

"I'll make a preacher of that boy," father declared. "I can see him in the pulpit wearing a black gown and warning them against the Devil and all his works. All he needs is a bit of Latin and Greek."

"There's nothin' like the church," chimed in the old soldier. Mother had retreated upstairs from what she regarded as an entertainment for drunk men.

Mr. Ansell began to be nostalgic.

"When I was with 'the Skins' in the Punjab," he began, "once the Colonel, he says to me—oh a fine gentleman from Limavady he was—well, as I was saying, the Colonel he says, 'Corporal Ansell' ..."

By this time I was feeling drowsy, for it was past my normal bedtime, and the Colonel's words were lost forever. I bade the two men goodnight and climbed the stairs, candlestick in hand.

I slept at the top of the tall brick house and into my little room came the whine and grind of tramcars to-and-froing on the Newtownards Road. I heard, too, the diminishing shouts in the side streets of the workers' children. I watched the play of shadows on the wall while my mind turned to coming excitements. My friend Johnny Carson had asked me to a party where there was sure to be fizzy drinks and spongy cakes. Perhaps Johnny and I would go to the Picturedrome on Boxing Day to see Jeanette MacDonald and Nelson Eddy in *Rose Marie*. But, above all, I thought of powdery snowflakes and frozen ponds and the slides we would make in the narrow streets off the road. These for me were, after all, the streets of freedom. Snow would make them even more exciting.

I woke with a start to see mother standing beside my bed, crying softly into her dress.

"Get up, Robbie, and put on you," she whispered. "It's your granny. She's ..."

Father, mother and I hurried out into the night drizzle, down

54

Middlepath Street and over the Queen's Bridge, where only a few muffled phantoms slithered homewards and a bull-like lorry butted against the unfriendly night. Out of half-closed eyes, I saw the indistinct outline of the cross-channel vessels and then the hands of the Albert Clock.

Father ran over to the taxi rank and, in a moment, we were being driven smoothly up Great Victoria Street and towards Shaftesbury Square. The taxi was roomy and smelled of rich leather. The rain spat lazily against the windows. The taxi driver was saying something about the Christmas displays in the shops, but his words petered out for lack of response.

The house of death was crowded with neighbours huddled together in the gas-lit kitchen. Some of them drank tea out of enamel mugs and spoke in conspiratorial tones. The air was thick and tense. A bearded old fellow smoked a pipe, emitting fumes at random and mouthing something about God and mercy. My aunts appeared, spare Aunt Annie and plump Aunt Tillie, both red-eyed. A clock ticked with busy insolence. My parents and I tiptoed upstairs. We passed the sitting room where I had practised scales and where hung the painting of the old farmhouse in County Tyrone where granny had been a girl. We passed the print of the stag-at-bay on the landing and went into the room of the dead woman.

Aunt Annie opened the door and then burst into tears. "Here she is," she whimpered, "the best mother anyone ever had." I looked at the stiff figure that had already been washed and laid out. The dead woman's hands rested on a Bible, those hands that had both punished me with a tawse for naughtiness and rewarded me with silver coins for virtue. I felt myself gasping for breath, unable to transform my feelings into words. It was as if the angel of death were still loitering in the room. I wondered how I ought to behave. Such a situation was outside my experience.

Back in the kitchen, the smell of death was still in my nostrils. I glanced at the assembled faces that looked as if they had been sprayed yellow by the gaslight. I noticed the food stains on the old man's beard. Then the old man sat up with a start, for there was a loud rapping at the door. Aunt Tillie rushed to it. I heard a voice and caught some of the words: " ... told me the sad news ... come to offer ..."

A man came in. "This is Mr. Clarke," said Aunt Tillie. "I'm sure some of you know him."

There was a ragged chorus of helloing and come-in-out-of-the-wet-mister. I had seen the stranger once or twice before. I took in the grey cloth cap, the long trailing muffler and the wrinkled, paint-splashed macintosh. I had heard this man described as 'Bolshy', whatever that was.

"That's a cruel night, friends, so it is," said Mr. Clarke, wiping his forehead with a big handkerchief.

"It is now, to be sure," agreed father, making way for the newcomer.

"I wouldn't put a dog out in it."

"Would you like a cup of tea?" asked Aunt Tillie.

"I wouldn't say no to a wee drop," said Mr. Clarke.

The bearded man stirred and heaved himself erect in his chair.

"She's up in heaven now," he said, lifting his eyes piously and fixing them on the ceiling like a street evangelist trying to attract a crowd.

"What's that you said?" asked Mr. Clarke sharply.

"I said she's up in heaven now, good Christian that she was," replied the bearded man.

"A good woman, yes I agree with that," answered Mr. Clarke, "but that stuff about heaven and harps is a fairy tale for wee childer."

There was a stunned silence and then a roar from the bearded one.

"How dare you deny your Maker," he screamed. "How dare you! You Russian atheist! God might strike you dead this minute for your blasphemy."

Everyone was now in a timeless vacuum. Silence reigned. The tick of the clock came loud and clear.

"Then let Him strike me dead," said Mr. Clarke calmly. "I'll give Him exactly sixty seconds to do it."

The old man's beard trembled with passion as if every white hair in it had been individually insulted.

"No wonder they call you Bolshy, you Russian pig," shouted the old man.

The word 'pig' had barely been pronounced when Mr. Clarke's fist struck the nose of the bearded Christian. "Pig yourself!" retorted Mr. Clarke. "Now men, steady on," cried father, somewhat indecisively.

But my two aunts had by now leaped to their feet almost simultaneously. Aunt Annie clutched the old man and Aunt Tillie held Mr. Clarke's arm in a vice-like grip.

"Now that's as much from either of you as I want to listen to," said Aunt Tillie firmly. "My poor mother is lying dead upstairs and all you two can do is to start fighting. Two grown up men, you should be ashamed of yourselves."

The two offenders muttered apologies and seated themselves at some distance from each other. The sixty seconds Mr. Clarke had given his Creator to strike him dead were long up. I was surprised that Mr. Clarke was still breathing, but God I knew was merciful to miserable sinners. "It's time you were in bed, Robbie," said mother. "Come along now, you've had more excitement this night than is good for you."

I lay awake a long time in a strange bed after mother had kissed me goodnight. It would soon be Christmas. Would there be snow? I prayed to God for snow. Then the image of my dead granny came into my mind and I felt guilty for having thought first of snow. Suppose there was no heaven as Mr. Clarke had maintained? But I knew that Mr. Clarke was wrong. Granny must be in heaven.

As I drifted into sleep, I saw the flakes falling and settling on the beard of the old man, so that the food stains were cancelled out and the beard was immaculately white. The beard gradually turned into a tombstone. A dark bird flew to the tombstone and perched on it. Then it started to peck at the stone with its beak.

It did this until granny's name and her dates of birth and death appeared. Suddenly there was a flash of lightning that lit up the graveyard and then a thunder clap. The tombstone dissolved. Next I saw the old man with the beard flying heavenwards. Dangling from the end of a rope was the limp body of Mr. Clarke wrapped in his wrinkled macintosh the muffler flying in the wind. Out of his mouth there issued thick black coils of smoke.

In the days that followed, carollers appeared in the streets, shop windows were decorated with bits of cotton wool to simulate snow and people hurried along with bulging baskets and parcels wrapped in coloured paper. But I kept remembering that granny was dead and that we had driven into the heart of Tyrone to bury her at Leckpatrick. Mr. Clarke had not been among the mourners. Had God struck him dead after all? I did not care.

When I woke on the morning of Christmas Day, I jumped out of bed and ran eagerly to the window. There was no snow on the ground, so my prayers had gone unanswered. But at least the ground and windows were frosted. Even in my room the air had a nip in it, a fresh edge that was exhilarating. I looked everywhere for a present but could not find one.

Father and I hurried off to church after breakfast, but I had no ears for the hymns and psalms and the long-winded sermon. The absence of a present, or any mention of one to come, kept nagging. Outside church the air sparkled in the winter sunshine. I asked father to let me go for a wee run and he dismissed me with the warning not to be late for dinner. "We've got a big fat goose from Monaghan," he said. I knew it had been sent to us by his sister Liz-Ann.

I headed towards the Holywood Arches, running and jumping with relief that the church service was over. I had gone only a few hundred yards when I bumped into Fat Wilson and Willie Anderson. Fat was resplendent in new kid gloves and swinging his arms as if to demonstrate his superiority. Willie, a pale, stunted boy—did he smoke butt ends of cigarettes picked up in the gutter?—hopped along beside Fat like a sparrow trying to keep on friendly terms with a pigeon.

"Hi there, you! Does yer ma know you're out the day?" was Fat's cheeky greeting. Willie chuckled obsequiously at the sally.

Unable to think of a suitable riposte, I said lamely, "We've got a goose, a big one."

"Did you ever hear the like of that, Willie?" demanded Fat removing his left glove with calculated elegance. "Sure everybody except the riff-raff has a turkey at Christmas. We've got a turkey and two chickens and lots of sausages and mince pies and *everything*."

"My old man bought a turkey in the market," said Willie, probably lying.

"Them's nice gloves," I said to Fat in an attempt at appeasement.

"'Nice', says he," retorted Fat. "You mean them's the best bloody gloves money could buy in this city or even in London." But worse was to come.

"What have you got for Christmas?" he asked. Malice shone out of his piggy eyes. "I've got ... I've got ... " I stammered, "a pair of roller skates."

"Liar! Liar! Liar!" answered Fat, who had shrewdly noted my hesitation. Then he rubbed salt into the wound. "I can't see that hopeless old da of yours buying you anything. Doesn't he spend all his money on drink in McMahon's?"

I blushed.

"Well," I said loyally, "he spends his own money. He doesn't borrow from anybody."

Fat snorted contemptuously. He knew he had won. Now he ignored me.

"Come on, Willie," he said. "Come on back with me for a couple of hot mince pies."

Upset, I was left standing on the pavement. It was as if the crisp air had gone soggy and clammy and the bright sky had suddenly darkened. I thought for a moment it was going to rain and even stretched out my hand to feel the first raindrops, before I realised that I had fallen into a dream state.

I was late for dinner.

"What have you been up to?" mother asked crossly. The goose was already being carved, but the normal high spirits of a family gathered round the table on Christmas Day were singularly absent. Granny's recent death weighed on us all.

I listened moodily to the conversation and only vaguely heard the words of my parents as they spoke of Christmases long before I was born. I day-dreamed of how I might borrow a pair of skates so that I could rush past nasty old Fat and shove him into the gutter and then push the contemptible Willie on top of him. Revenge was sweet.

"What's wrong with you today?" asked father, with a little bit more concern in his voice than usual. "Don't you like the goose? It seems tender enough to me."

"The goose is fine," I said with a marked lack of enthusiasm.

"Are you grieving for your granny?" asked mother.

"Only a wee bit," I said truthfully. "You see ... you see ... I met Fat Wilson up the road and he was boasting and showing-off as usual. He said some horrible things to me and Willie Anderson was backing him up."

"Don't let it worry you," said mother.

"Well," said father, after swallowing a dollop of stuffing, "if he goes on like that you'll have to use your fists on him one of these fine days."

"Now don't encourage the child to fight," said mother.

Father put his hand in his pocket and drew out a fistful of coins. He selected one. "We hadn't time to buy you anything for Christmas, what with all the upset over granny. Take this and buy yourself something." I took the shilling he offered and put it—with a polite word of thanks—into my hip pocket. I was not pleased with the gift.

I asked permission to go out for a walk. Having crossed the city, I went over to the south side. I made my way up University

Road, passed the Museum and Art Gallery on the Stranmillis Road and headed in the direction of the Lagan tow-path. I had thought of calling at Johnny Carson's house. Johnny always stood by me and might even have helped in planning revenge on Fat. But I felt I could not unburden myself, not even to Johnny. I knew that Fat would spread the news of his encounter with me and tell others that I was a liar. *One day* ... I thought ... *one day* ... and I clenched my fists.

I felt an anger, a turbulence within me that was at odds with the season of peace and goodwill. Coming to a bridge, I leaned over the parapet and looked dully at the moving water. Almost before I knew what I was doing, I pulled the shilling out of my pocket and threw it into the river. I shivered at the recklessness of what I had done and a tear trickled down my cheek. I started the trek home. As I neared the straggle of houses at the city's edge, the lights were going up one by one. I started to whistle, whether to cheer myself up or because the tension had gone, I did not rightly know.

SIX

Waiting for Lefty

In September 1933, at the age of thirteen, I left the school in Templemore Avenue and made my début in the Lower Fourth at the Methodist College in Belfast. I was over-awed by the sense of purpose, organisation and the sheer size of everything. Obviously one had gone there to *work*, not to enjoy a rest-cure. The first few days were tough and bewildering. Yet it was clear that discipline would not be imposed by the slaughter-house methods of the primary school where caning was an everyday occurrence. No, there was not a cane in sight at Methody and not one of the masters looked like a butcher. Nonetheless, these gowned and learned figures had an indefinable air of authority. They were *masters* in the real sense of the word, and would stand no nonsense. Or would they? I decided to play it safe.

At Templemore Avenue, my teaches had all been Ulstermen, mostly local men at that. We spoke the same dialect more or less, and shared practically all the same assumptions; and our prejudices largely coincided. Here at Methody a high proportion of the staff were Englishmen, Scots and Welshmen. The headmaster, an awe-inspiring, Jehovah-like person, was a Scot named Henderson. The next in command, Mr. John Falconer (also a Scot) pulsated with energy. It was Mr. Falconer who was in charge of the Lower Fourth, the newcomers—apart from a handful of boys who had been at the Methody prep school,

Downey House—so to some extent we judged all the masters by Mr. Falconer. Within minutes the brighter among the new recruits knew somehow that he was called 'The Hawk' and had a reputation for severity tempered with justice. It was whispered that he was all right if you obeyed him. If you failed him, you were for it; and if you 'cheeked' him, heaven help you! The Hawk certainly put the fear of God into me, if not into one or two rougher, more insolent lads. Commands issued in that resonant Scots voice were given to be obeyed—or else!

The Hawk and I were to come into conflict on very few occasions. Yet collide we did—and I always got the worst of it. I could not complain that he had been the least bit unfair, even in his punishment. If a boy were not guilty he need have no fear in stating his case to 'Johnny' Falconer. He lashed me with his tongue on at least two occasions when I had been guilty of an offence—once when I had cut my name on a desk, and once when I had been discovered talking to another boy at prayers in morning assembly. I heard of only one boy who had actually dared to be insolent to The Hawk, a vicious boy whom I had reason to dislike and who was later expelled for, I believe, breaking a window deliberately. I may say that Mr. Falconer, in my later years at Methody, more or less indicated his friendly interest in my literary ambitions. As editor of the school magazine, *M.C.B.*, he was to publish my early efforts in verse and prose. Mr. Falconer became headmaster after my time, but even in that exalted position I doubt whether he appeared more impressive to my successors in the Lower Fourth than he did to my contemporaries.

It was a strange sensation to be associating with potential young gentlemen. That is not to say they were above larking about or throwing their weight around. On a few occasions there were real stand-up fights, but these were rare. More often there were scuffles in the locker room or threats exchanged in a half-humorous, half-angry tone. The manliness of these boys did not consist in simple punching and kicking, but took on subtler guises. A tiny few were determined to make their mark both academically and on the sports field. Some were scholars pure and simple. Others looked forward mainly to the shove and thrust of rugger. Most were undistinguished on the playing field or in the classroom; but, out of these, certain boys had individual interests they pursued with intensity. The really stupid were as rare as the really brilliant, through one wondered about a handful of lads how they managed to be let in at all. Had a guardian angel stood at their right hand and guided the pen with which they wrote their English essays and coped with their mathematical problems?

For myself, I went to Methody full of resolves for hard work and giving as little trouble as possible to those whom God had ordained as my superiors. As the years passed, alas! and as conditions at home became more and more strained, I took to inward (rather than outward) rebellion. *Non serviam* became my motto. I later did less and less work, except at those subjects, like English and History, in which I could do fairly well, anyhow, with a minimum of effort. I had rebelled against sport after the first two or three years so that, by the time I had reached the upper forms, I had gracelessly bowed myself out of that arena. (One of my problems on the sports field was my indifferent eyesight. Should I take my glasses off and see badly, or keep them on and risk having them broken? Another problem was that I longed to be more than just another mediocre player. Yet I knew I was no giant, no Colquohoun or Grimshaw.) At Science and Mathematics, I was indifferent, so the only thing for me was to be 'literary'. What else could I do well? By the age of sixteen I was beginning to send out an occasional article and poem here and there, for I felt I could only find myself in verbal self-expression. And so it has proved. That process of 'finding myself' has continued to this day—and it is a process that will end only with death.

At thirteen, then, I first entered the dewy world of infinite possibility. Eagerly I joined in work and play and friendship. It was all so simple. Life was there for the grasping. Go on, grasp it, Robert! Doubt and rebellion came with adolescence. But as I write, well advanced in years, I think my sympathies have returned to my thirteen-year-old, enthusiastic self. The world is indeed there for the taking, if only we have the courage not be dismayed by apparent, yet often unreal, difficulties. In his *Margin Released*, J.B. Priestley remarks on the importance of character for anyone who wants to become and stay a writer. In youth one tends to over-rate talent and under-rate those qualities of grit and determination and courage in the face of odds that we sum up in the word 'character'. Of one thing I am certain—and that is the futility of taking the advice of others in important matters. Similarly, I believe the advice of others can be immensely useful in coping with minor affairs. These truths, however, were only to come with the years; and they had to be bitterly paid for.

Neither truly introverted or extroverted, I found little difficulty in making friends. Among boys there tends to be quick shifts in friendship, for they enjoy playing at what one might call social politics. Alliances form, dissolve and new patterns come into being. The close friend of a thirteen-year-old may be forgotten in three years' time. We are, of course, inevitably drawn to those with whom we share interests yet who are unlike us in temperament. Optimist and pessimist consort together. During my first few weeks at Methody, I made a number of new friends, but only one of them who was to last a lifetime. That was Leslie Baxter, a tall, unusually helpful, well-mannered serious boy with a strong vocation for teaching. I do not think that Leslie and I have been at all alike temperamentally; nor have our interests and ideas coincided. One of our bonds has been our common interest in the arts. When Leslie left school he went to the College of Art in Belfast—an institution which was then, it always seemed to me, to be unfittingly housed in the 'Tech' building—and there qualified as an art teacher, making a subsequent career for himself in that field. Unlike me, he has not been tempted to stray from his native place, apart from making summer excursions to continental art galleries and churches. What a pub crawl is to other men a church (or cathedral) crawl is to a person like Leslie Baxter!

It would be invidious to pick out the names of boys with whom friendship suddenly ripened and then, more often than not, ceased equally suddenly, and for no very obvious reason. That is the way of young animals not yet set in their ways. A boy with whom friendship extended beyond school was Ernest Baird, who shared my enthusiasm for books. Often at his home we discussed our reading into the small hours—I remember how amused we once were when we came across a remark of Arnold Bennett's (was it about a novel by the Scottish writer, Lewis Grassic Gibbon?) to the effect: "It cannot not be a classic." We found Bennett's *Literary Taste* a useful signpost to further reading.

Oddly enough I was to meet some Methody boys later on and I am glad to say the old school has produced a number of writers of more than local fame, and whom I counted among my friends. Of these I would mention John Hewitt, poet, art critic and man of letters and another poet, Richard Kell. It is a pity that Hewitt, Kell and I were not contemporaries. What a stimulating effect we would have had on each other!

I can remember getting into one serious 'scrape' at Methody, but have only the vaguest memory of the details. Even at the time I found myself implicated in happenings I did not fully understand. I was a case of the 'innocent bystander' being hit by a bullet. Some sort of rough-housing was apparently going on in the vicinity of the locker room and lavatory. Within minutes The Hawk had swooped the eponymous bird of prey. "See he-rrr-e me boy ..." he began. A group of boys, of whom I was one, was swiftly rounded up, caught in the act. Neither then or now do I know what the act happened to be! Protestations of innocence with regard to whatever mischief had been afoot were to no avail. The only other boy I remember being implicated was Ernest Paul, whom I knew well then and afterwards. We were all suspended for an indefinite period. What would happen? Would we all be expelled? It was all the more ghastly for me since I had little idea of what it was all about. If I had been clearly guilty I could have owned up. As it was, my general feeling of guilt had been aroused and I was a bit like one of those Russians during the Stalinist era who were prepared, after brain-washing, to write full confessions about crimes they had not committed. Of one thing I was sure—I ought not to have been out of my classroom at the time I was caught. A minor offence had rapidly become a major one. As usual I set off for school each morning—not having breathed a word of the suspension to any outsider—but, being barred from classes, simply mooched around the grounds with some of my fellow-culprits or wandered listlessly and aimlessly through the city streets. Expulsion from Methody was not be taken lightly. The others involved in the offence would not talk about it, so the mystery thickened. One day I was told by an assistant master that, if I wrote an apology, it had a chance of acceptance; he gave me a general outline of what I might say. It was all up to the headmaster ... there was no guarantee that the apology would be accepted.

I began a letter, hinting at guilt but not quite admitting it and beginning 'Dear Headmaster'. A day passed and I prayed as I had never prayed before. But the prayer was answered. I was pardoned, and only a few of the real culprits punished. Nobody was expelled. A chastened Robert went back to classes. The whole experience made me doubt the validity of the concept of justice, yet I clung as best I could to the idea that in the end the innocent would come out with no mark against their names. It had been horrible, however, to have been in a position where one had appeared to be guilty of some unknown offence. I decided one not only had to be innocent, but to be clearly seen to be innocent. No doubt the headmaster, Mr. Henderson, realised that the boys caught by The Hawk were not truly wicked or insolent. I certainly had no criminal record. Back at classes I realised that I had a certain glamour, especially for the average boy who probably supposed I had done something really naughty and had survived it. I had come through the fire unscathed after all. I settled down as quickly as I could to humdrum anonymity— even though I did nurse a certain sullen and hidden discontent—all heroism spent. Just as earlier I had played the role of The Boy Who Had Nearly Died now I played that of The Boy

Who Had Nearly Been Expelled. At least it lifted one out of the common run, though I knew it would never to do to get a reputation for being a bad 'un.

Examinations could be a nightmare. After the expulsion threat for a time I was unusually quiet and industrious, but soon I was in a rebellious mood again. As notions of revolt grew in me, industry decreased, and I followed my own devices more and more. The result was that I came to fear exams—end of term exams, Junior and then Senior—for which I knew myself, in some subjects, to be ill-equipped. This was all the more devastating since my masters kept telling me I could do really well if I tried. But why should I? Unusually energetic in some ways I gradually drifted into being an idler academically, with the result that in most exams I just managed to scrape through, except in one or two subjects I found easy. The only piece of homework I started to take seriously was the weekly essay which increasingly became a labour of delight. I took pleasure in being deliberately exhibitionist and outrageous in my essays, setting off squibs for all I was worth—squibs that frequently expressed left-wing, free-love, and violently anti-bourgeois opinions that no doubt seldom found their ways into the essays of Belfast grammar school boys.

My masters, however, were exceptionally tolerant, I must say. They probably realised that I was having a more than normally disturbed adolescence. Having discovered D.H. Lawrence's *Sons and Lovers*, I became a devoted Laurentian; and my admiration for Lawrence the writer, if not the thinker, has never really cooled. James Joyce was soon added to the figures in my private gallery of the truly great of the twentieth century. Is it surprising, in view of what I have already written about my adolescence, that my admiration was given so unstintingly to two life-long rebels, who, like me, had early decided they would not serve that in which they had ceased to believe? I remember one of my masters expressing shock and surprise when he read in the school magazine an article that expressed my interest in D.H. Lawrence. Perhaps, for him, Lawrence just seemed the abominable author of the then whispered-about *Lady Chatterley's Lover*. Yet Mr. Falconer, more tolerant than the more 'advanced' boys would have supposed, was willing to print my views—in a slightly toned-down form—in, of all journals, *M.C.B.* Perhaps I was not so unlucky in my school after all.

Among the masters who impressed me there was one I came to admire, almost love, when I reached the higher forms. That was Ronnie Marshall, a Cambridge aesthete—or so he seemed to me—who taught English and History. Ronnie had a sophistication I had never come across before and it appealed to me forcibly. Immaculate in his appearance, arresting in expression (enhanced with a slight lisp) of at times somewhat unconventional views, Ronnie treated us not as pimply schoolboys but as intellectual equals. That, I think, is what endeared him to me. One did not have the impression of an adult 'talking down' as with some of the other masters. He seemed to be saying, as it were: "Well, you are all old enough now to form your own opinions. Go ahead and do so. I'm here to give you the background of fact on which to base them." Not least impressive was that Ronnie was an Italophile, who spoke Italian fluently and had made a special study of Italian history. Perhaps my liking for *pasta* comes from his influence, as also my contempt for the mob, which he used to describe so breath-takingly as 'the Great Unwashed'.

Rebellion did not just take a negative form and was not just a matter of being against all forms of authority. I had chanced to come into contact with a group of young Queen's graduates who told me of the exciting new developments in Russia, or, as they preferred to say, the Soviet Union, a country that was proud to call itself 'One Sixth of the Earth'. They assured me that reports about concentration camps not so very different from the Nazi model, and the extermination of the Kulaks and minority peoples were lies—plain capitalist lies—and that our newspapers had to build up the Red Bogey. What else, they insisted, *would* our newspapers say? I began to read the *Daily Worker* and the yellow-orange covered Left Book Club books they lent me; I tried manfully to read Marx's *Capital* but shame-facedly gave up. I found the *Communist Manifesto* easy going and thrilled to the sentiment: "There is a spectre haunting Europe ... the spectre of Communism." "Workers of the world unite, you have nothing to lose but your chains" began to seem more and more true.

If we do not stop the Nazis in Germany and the Italian Fascists, said my new friends, humanity is lost. The clouds darkened in Spain and the Spanish Civil War was upon us. That Franco was supported by the Roman Catholic Church did not seem a good omen to Protestant Ulstermen. 'No Pasaran' became a slogan as real to me as the 'Remember 1690' scrawled or painted on gables. Mass action! On Guard for Spain! A Popular Front Now! Chamberlain Must Go! Workers of Hand and Brain Unite!

All is not yet lost, urged my new mentors, whom I met with pleasurable eagerness. We have friends in high places, they said. Don't worry, we can eventually capture the citadels of power in the Labour Movement. I became more and more interested in these new and stimulating ideas. Who gave a damn for Senior Certificate when there was a world to be lost and a world to be won? Instead of doing my homework in those last anxious years of the 30s, I would sneak of an evening to some out-of-the-way hall and listen to a Marxist analyse the current situation. Or I would go to watch a Soviet film made by Pudovkin or Eisenstein, or see some plays such as Clifford Odets' *Waiting for Lefty*. Or in the vastness of my little bedroom-*cum*-study I would read the stirring political poems of Auden and Spender and C. Day Lewis. I could indeed hear the 'opening of a new theme'. Bliss it was in that Red Dawn to be alive and to be young was a veritable Soviet heaven.

Within a year or two, I was to be sadly disillusioned by it all. The dream crumbled before the iron realities like the Soviet-German pact and the disclosures of savage Stalinist repression of the kind that came to be openly admitted by Soviet leaders. The god had failed. But, at that time, disillusion and bitterness and quarrels with former friends who still believed was not yet. For the time being there was blinding new light in eastern Europe, and it was spreading a crimson glow over the sleeping west. Awake! Awake! Even in faction-ridden, obscurantist Belfast, if one peered closely into the heavens, it was possible to discern the proud Red Star. It could shine for us, too, and the Lagan could flow crimson.

All this time, during this new surge of hope—days and nights of it—I was going to Methody as usual and being as discreet as possible about my views to my elders and betters, some of whom would have been angry, while others would have merely laughed. At Methody, however, I found a few boys who were willing to sympathise and read the subversive literature I smuggled in. This was read with as much zest as other lads showed in poring over pornography. Soon I would be a man, I thought, and able to play my part on the stage of the big world. Even schooldays must come to an end. Then I would set the Lagan on fire. O dreams, O destinations!

SEVEN

Heroes This Way

Johnston was a big fellow with slouching movements and slow speech. He was determined to be a boss. A good sportsman, he captained the junior rugby team and would one day, everyone believed, be captain of the 1st XV, which in itself conferred heroic status. His academic performance was mediocre. Nobody liked him particularly, but it would be untrue to say that he was hated. Though feared, he harmed nobody so long as he was not crossed. Cross him and, once his slow mind had decided what was to be done, he would surely do it in his own apparently lazy yet determined way.

It must have been in my second year at Methody that I became aware of Johnston. Nobody called him by his Christian name, Julian, perhaps because it was the only Julian one had heard of. He was Johnston and nothing else. That was the name he scrawled on his exercise books. If he came into the locker room for his books, he elbowed everyone else aside, definitely but not viciously. If you had already opened your locker drawer and were sorting out books or gear, you automatically made way and let Johnston go ahead. It was an unwritten rule.

Johnston said no word of thanks, but took it as a *droit de seigneur*. He had a natural ascendency over other boys, even over clever, quick-witted boys. "When I'm captain of the 1st XV ... " he would drawl. Johnston had an uncanny feeling of rightness even when he was dead wrong. He once disputed the spelling of a word with the English master, who proved Johnston wrong by pointing out to him the word in a dictionary. Johnston would not admit his mistake. "I know it as a fact," he announced, and some of his toadies agreed that the dictionary must be wrong. Perhaps they were hoping for a place in the 1st XV one day.

I remember that, in the locker room, a boy called McAllister said to Johnston, "I was here first and I'm in a hurry". Johnston stopped and looked hard at him.

"What did you say?" Johnston did not always quite get it first time.

"I said I was here before you and that I'm in a hurry."

"So you're in a hurry," said Johnston, emphasising every word. "Are those your books?"

"Yes", said McAllister.

"Give them to me."

McAllister meekly handed a pile of books to Johnston. Johnston held them above his head like a rugby ball and then flung them with all his might into the far corner of the locker room. Now McAllister, who was no coward—I had seen him fight valiantly— said nothing but walked away defeated. He never challenged Johnston again.

Another place dominated by Johnston was the bicycle shed. Five or ten minutes before morning assembly, the shed would be a seething mass of boys dismounting and storing away their bicycles. One morning, Johnston arrived just as another boy was putting his bike into position in the spot Johnston generally chose.

"That's *my* place," said Johnston.

"Then why didn't you get here before me?" asked the other boy.

"That's *my* place," repeated Johnston.

The boy walked off before Johnston could think of what to do next.

I knew slightly the pale, dark-haired boy who had dared to displease Johnston. He was a newcomer to the school, one Clive

Dunton, a boy from Lancashire whose father was a Salvation Army major. Dunton was a bit of a dandy with oiled hair and beautifully-creased pants. Johnston was not in the habit of bothering to address nonentities like myself, but he was obviously crestfallen. He turned to me and said, "I won't take cheek from anybody and least of all from that oily English bugger". I nodded, for I had no wish to be involved. I had enough problems to occupy my attention.

At break I looked around for Johnston, for I expected he would be on the prowl for Dunton with a view to physical rather than verbal aggression. Not so, for Johnston lay sprawled on the steps of the canteen, surrounded by several admiring younger boys and deep in conversation with his crony, Dick Watters. Watters was a sly fellow. He flattered Johnston and carried out little jobs that Johnston wanted done, but was too important or lazy to do for himself.

When I went, after school, to pick up my bike, Johnston and Watters were hanging round. They watched several boys push off home. Watters came over to me.

"Would you like to see a little bit of fun?" he asked.

"Fun? What sort of fun?" I asked.

"Just a wee bit of fun," said Watters with a grin.

I should have jumped on my bike that minute and made off. I watched with Watters while Johnston put his hand in his pocket and pulled out a razor blade. He flashed the blade in the sunshine with a Byronic gesture before walking over to the bike that had been stowed away in the wrong place, *his* place. Slash! Slash! Slash! He ripped both tyres with a few beautifully co-ordinated movements. I could not help admiring his dexterity though the deed appalled me.

Watters laughed and clapped his hands. "What happened just now?" he demanded.

"Johnston slashed the tyres of Dunton's bike." It was obvious, surely.

"What big eyes you have, granny," said Watters sharply. He reached towards me and pulled my glasses off.

"How handsome you are, granny," said Johnston. "Ask him the question again."

"What happened just now?" Watters asked. "Think before you reply."

A minute passed before I could bring myself to give the answer required.

"Nothing," I said.

"You're not as stupid as I thought," said Watters. "Give him back his glasses," said Johnston.

Watters pushed the glasses roughly into my hands.

"Bugger off," said Johnston.

Next morning the headmaster, after prayers, said he had a special announcement to make. He spoke of "unparalleled hooliganism ... great discourtesy to a new boy and a stranger to our city ... duty to the school ... the community". We filed out. The words buzzed in my head. Johnston was getting away with too much. Big-headed bully. Bullies should not get away with it. The headmaster was right, though I generally thought him a pompous ass. I would tell. Yes, I would tell.

The bell released me into the clamour of tuckshop and playground. I walked along the corridor, head down. *Must tell.* Suddenly, Johnston and Watters appeared.

"Going for a walk?" Watters enquired.

"Heroes this way," said Johnston, seizing my arm and dragging me into an empty classroom.

"Why don't you own up?" I said weakly. "You heard what the headmaster said at Assembly."

"He only heard one side of the story," said Watters, as if he were Johnston's lawyer. "He only heard what the Salvationist swine had to tell him. Bloody foreigner. I'll bet he didn't say a word about being offensive to Johnston."

Johnston looked at me.

"You hear what Watters says," he said.

Johnston put his hand in his pocket and pulled out a tin box that had once held tobacco flakes. He opened it slowly and took out a razor blade.

"This is sharp," he said. "A beautiful edge. Best quality Sheffield steel."

Watters grinned in his nasty way. "High time you started shaving," he said.

"Ask him some questions, Watters," said Johnston.

"Did you see anything interesting yesterday?" asked Watters. "At the cycle shed, say?"

There was a long pause while Johnston stroked the razor blade.

"I don't think so," I replied.

Johnston and Watters laughed. They walked off together and left me standing there nervously. I can still hear their laughter as they ran down the corridor and out into the playground.

EIGHT

Butterfly

Butterfly may seem a strange name for a hefty schoolboy with black hairs on his wrists, a larger-than-average head and blue eyes that gazed into infinite space. James Walter Brown was his real name but we always called him Butterfly because he had written in a composition: "A bat is a sort of big blind butterfly." Even if Butterfly had given a definition of 'bat' equal to that in the *Concise Oxford Dictionary*, we would have sniggered anyway and said he had copied it from a book. We never allowed Butterfly to win, as, by consensus of schoolboy opinion, Butterfly was only one remove from being an idiot.

Big and shambling, neither at home in classroom nor playing field—and not even when larking around the locker room where our small dramas were enacted—Butterfly was an odd boy out. Those of us who were none too sure of our own place in the hierarchy knew one fact for sure: Butterfly was at the bottom of the form and he was going to stay there. One might not be awfully bright, but one was brighter than that big slob.

Funny when you thought about it, because Stewart was really dense, but if you hinted at his denseness you would most likely get a vicious blow in the groin. Dixon kicked a ball like a girl and actually enjoyed the academic grind, but you dared not offend him or he would not lend a hand with Latin homework. I could cobble sentences together and so make a little knowledge go a

77

long way, and as a result was in demand as a writer of letters to the headmaster that were supposed to come from parents. Truancies could be explained away as illnesses or family commitments. Many a boy owed me a debt of gratitude for having explained how he had to attend his grandfather's funeral in a remote village.

I was not a bully, yet I must confess that I sometimes bullied Butterfly in a mild sort of way. Sometimes, when the mood was on me, I defended him. I quite liked Butterfly in spite of his daft ways, but I had not the guts to stand up for him unequivocally. Life with father was difficult and schoolmasters could be demanding. I had no intention of seeking unnecessary attention of an unpleasant kind by being known as Butterfly's friend. An appearance of conformity paid—so the class butt had to stay the class butt. All groups have their scapegoats and Butterfly was ours.

One Saturday afternoon, I had actually visited Butterfly's home, though naturally I did not breathe a word about that to any of the lads. I was glad to go there, for none of the others ever bothered to ask me. Butterfly's house turned out to be a suburban one just beyond the end of the Malone Road. It was sizeable compared with the house I lived in and had a nice big garden. Real middle class, I thought, but a bit gloomy and smelling of Jeyes' disinfectant. Butterfly's old man had money somewhere and, in the world I was familiar with, money brought admiration—you had prospered, so God was on your side. Of course, that was before I had turned fully into a red-hot socialist and thought it terribly wrong to have money wrung out of the downtrodden workers.

Butterfly's father was a stout man with a large moustache. He had a resonant voice that suggested self-confidence, yet the voice sounded a trifle gloomy and monotonous in tone. I remember his telling me how he had started work as an office boy at five shillings a week. There's money in fruit, I thought, that's where it comes from. All those oranges and apples and bananas have brought in the money.

The father asked me what books I read. I mentioned a few and thought he would be impressed that I had dipped into writers as different as Forrest Reid—who lived somewhere in our city, it was said—Hardy and D.H. Lawrence. He too had looked at the work of these writers, but found them wanting one way and another. Then he said, a trifle ponderously: "In my view, Somerset Maugham's the greatest writer alive—and do you know why?'

"No, I don't," I replied, wondering whether I should have added 'sir'. I wanted to be correct and amiable. He smiled. Then came the explanation.

"Maugham," he said, "understands human beings with all their foibles yet he doesn't judge them. You ought to look at *Of Human Bondage* and some of his short stories. As for *The Summing Up*, I must have read it half-a-dozen times."

Now my English master (whose lisping Oxford accent I had tried to imitate) had once dismissed Somerset Maugham in the withering phrase—"the Austin Reed of literature". Actually, I rather coveted the clothes I saw in our local Austin Reed branch, for their sports jackets and grey worsted trousers seemed exquisite. I knew there must be something wrong with my taste both in books and clothes. The English master was for me a hero of culture and I knew he could not possibly be wrong. So I nodded my head sagely when Mr. Brown told me I should read Maugham. Snobbishly, I recalled that, after all, he had once been an office boy.

"Come and look at the flowers," said Mr. Brown, as if to indicate that the literary seminar had ended. I was not very interested in flowers as we had no garden at home, but I had manners enough to tell him that they were very nice. Then we talked about this and that, and laughed over a statement of a local MP who had said at Stormont that he was "walking hand in hand with the floodgates of democracy". Eventually, the conversation turned to the subject of Mr. Brown's son. One sentence is still in my mind: "I know I can rely on you to help Jim all you can."

Jim! I found it hard not to laugh. Imagine anyone calling

Butterfly *Jim!* I nodded gravely, feeling embarrassed. Mr. Brown was not only a grown-up but a rich grown-up who gave people orders in his office. Fruit importers who had money and large gloomy houses in the suburbs and flower gardens with exotic blooms and who admired W. Somerset Maugham both impressed and revolted me. Mr. Brown represented success. He had attained with a minimum of education what our teachers told us we must aim at. It was a puzzling old world.

I visited that house a few more times and, gradually, I came to have more respect for Mr. Brown. He was a widower and I supposed that the melancholy I detected in his voice was because he had no wife to look after him and Butterfly—Jim, I should say. He always gave me fruit to take home and mother was pleased that I had made friends with nice people who lived in a nice area in a nice big house. At school, I kept quiet about these visits and even adopted an aloof attitude towards Butterfly.

The real bully in our form was McKittrick. People said his father had been a docker before he went into the hardware business and that he beat McKittrick for the slightest misdemeanour. McKittrick obviously had to get his own back on somebody. He was an average-sized fifteen year old, dark and brooding. When he smiled you had to be on your guard. He struck without warning—and mercilessly. The more he hurt you, the better he was pleased. McKittrick seemed never to have heard of the schoolboy code of fair play that the majority of us observed. I had a bad quarter of an hour with him once, before I lost my temper and struck out. It led to a fight but, after that, McKittrick left me alone.

Fortunately for me, McKittrick slipped during the fight, so I came out of it reasonably well with only a cut lip. But he did manage to land several savage punches that had hurt. I thanked God for the metal tip on McKittrick's heel that made him slip. As I say, he left me alone after that punch-up, but he was still on the lookout for victims.

One day, Mr. Philipps gave us quadratic equations to get on with while he marked test papers. McKittrick was sitting directly

80

behind Butterfly. I had finished a couple of questions and felt I could take a well-earned rest without getting into trouble. I started looking round the class and making grimaces at one or two of my friends, just to see what would happen.

Then my eye caught McKittrick who was in the act of jabbing Butterfly in the small of the back with a heavy ruler. Butterfly turned round and tried to focus his blue eyes on his tormentor. This gave McKittrick the chance to take a swipe at a big bottle of blue-black *Stephens'* ink standing on Butterfly's desk (like many boys indifferent at schoolwork, Butterfly was fully equipped with the impedimenta of learning: pens, ink, rulers, geometrical instruments). The bottle fell right between Butterfly's legs. He jumped up with a muffled scream. I saw the ink trickle down the dark-grey regulation trousers.

Mr. Philipps looked up. His bushy eyebrows moved. He was clearly angry at being disturbed.

"Come up here, Brown," he shouted.

Butterfly shambled up to the master's desk. He nearly tripped over an undone shoelace.

"Look at yourself, Brown, you useless creature," said Mr. Philipps in his hoarse voice, half-contemptuous, half-friendly. "Just look at him, boys. Ready to join the army of the Great Unwashed."

We all laughed.

"But, sir ..." Butterfly began.

"But what?" enquired Mr. Philipps wearily.

"But, sir, I was attacked, sir. It wasn't my fault."

"You were attacked. Oh, indeed, and who was the aggressor, may I ask? Herr Hitler or Signor Mussolini?"

We all laughed again at the mention of these funny foreigners.

"Sir, McKittrick, sir. I think it was him."

"So you *think* it was McKittrick. It's fascinating to hear you have started *thinking*. Come up here, McKittrick!"

McKittrick marched up smartly, his face as innocent as a whitewashed wall.

"Did you attack Brown, McKittrick?"

"No, sir. Certainly not, sir," replied McKittrick in suitably outraged tones.

Mr. Philipps ignored the reply and addressed the class. "Did anyone see this alleged attack?"

I felt a shiver run through me. I looked down at the desk and the initials carved on it: W.L. As I gazed at the initials of some boy long gone from the school, I saw myself in the school yard near the bicycle shed, jacket off, facing McKittrick. I saw my friend, Dick Collins, holding my coat and books fastened by a leather strap. I heard Dick's enthusiastic voice as he jumped up and down and shouted encouragement to me, "Let him have it! Destroy him, Robert".

I talked silently to myself—"You saw the attack on Butterfly. *Tell! Tell!*" But my tongue stayed as if paralysed, useless, inert. *Tell! Tell!* I remained mute. McKittrick might not slip a second time and he would knock the guts out of me. After all, Butterfly was not a real friend. I sat rigid and gazed at the initials W.L. William Long? Wilfrid Lutton? Wesley Lang?

When we formed up in a jagged line to go into class after the lunch break, I heard a pathetic voice whisper down my neck, "You saw him do it. Why didn't you tell?" Butterfly looked more dishevelled and forlorn than ever. I felt guilty. Had not Mr. Brown invited me to his house and given me fruit to take home? Had he not asked me to help Butterfly all I could? I felt guilty, but also angry. The anger which should have been turned on McKittrick was deflected instead towards Butterfly. If he were not so stupid and useless, everything would be all right. Why didn't he stand up for himself, make an effort as I did? On impulse, I punched him in the ribs.

"I saw nothing," I shouted. "Nothing, I tell you. Butter-fingered Butterfly!"

A couple of days later, I went up to Butterfly and gave him a brown-papered parcel. It contained a big bottle of *Swan* ink I had bought out of my pocket money. "This is for you," I said. "I shouldn't have hit you. Sorry." He smiled weakly, mumbled his thanks and ambled off.

He never again asked me to visit his home and I never let anyone know I had ever done so. Even today, I sometimes think of Mr. Brown and his big gloomy house and the garden and the fruit and his interest in W. Somerset Maugham and the way he wanted me to help his son. Butterfly's almost inaudible words sound in my ears: "You saw him do it. Why didn't you tell?" If I could relive that incident all over again, would I have the courage to speak out? I'm afraid I don't know.

NINE

Waiting for Robert

Father was one of five children—John James, Robert, Henry, Elizabeth Ann and Samuel—born in the second marriage of a typical Presbyterian small farmer in County Monaghan. They moved two or three times, I believe, but for some years lived in the neighbourhood of Cootehill. A more prosperous and educated branch of the family had settled in the town of Monaghan—one of them was to become the chairman of the county council, but we never had any truck with grand folk of that kind. Father's name, incidentally, was Henry and it was given to me as a second Christian name, though plain Robert suits me fine. My paternal grandfather looked the patriarch, white goatee beard and all. I do not know what persona he presented to his sons and daughter, but on the occasions I saw him I regarded him with awe. He was a rural Jehovah, thunder-voiced, or, if not quite that, one of the immortals from Mount Olympus who had lived and ruled despotically for hundreds and hundreds of years.

In fact, I am not sure whether grandfather was as stern as all that, but that was the impression I had as a small boy. I avoided him as I would have avoided a collision with a big puff-puff. Father himself had, somehow or other, struggled out of the harshly frugal parental nest—though it did not strike me as being one of singing birds—and attempted to make his way in the narrow Ulster world with only a national school behind him and an early-developed, un-Presbyterian taste for liquor, a liking he never lost. (One of his brothers, my Uncle George, was a lifetime teetotaller, and the others only drank occasionally, at weddings or around Christmas.) "Many's the bit o' business was done over a wee drink," father used to say. Or again he would ask, "Would you tell me a clever man that couldn't take a drink?" A rhetorical question, indeed, to answer which would have invited a cuff on the ear. Mind you, when I got a bit older, I wanted to say: "Yes, Bernard Shaw—and he doesn't eat meat either! He's famous, too!" But I knew that father had no use for Bernard Shaw, whom he regarded as immoral, partly because he had written an exposure of his parents. Father had once said, "Imagine the oul' idiot makin' a laughin' stock of his own parents! He'll surely go till hell for it." Apparently, at the age of seventeen, father could down his whiskey with the best, or worst, of them. If success in business depended on a man's ability to drain his glass fast and often, then Henry Greacen's name would be inscribed far above that of Isaac Wolfson. Alas!

Father had tried farming without success. As his sister, my Aunt Liz-Ann—Elizabeth Ann—said, "Harry's heart was never in the moilin' and toilin'". That was only too clear. He wanted quick results. Crops would not grow fast enough or tall enough; prices in the market were never high enough; farming was a hard, dirty grind at which nobody grew rich. As a young man, he had tried his luck in one of those new-type creameries started by people like Sir Horace Plunkett and Æ as the basis of an Irish Rural Co-operative Movement. This work was more to father's liking. He enjoyed it and the prestige which came from being the manager of a creamery. He used to talk about a 'Father Poland' (that's what it sounded like but the name was probably Boland) he had been friendly with in those days, although father was normally somewhat suspicious of those who 'dug with the wrong foot'. Perhaps the priest was something of a Graham Greene character. I know that father was held in esteem in at least one of these jobs, for he always carried round with him a presentation gold-cased watch which had a copperplate inscription on the inside cover that referred, in a stiffly respectable phrase, to his qualities as a creamery manager. This watch was often consulted to know whether the pubs were about to open or shut. One of my early delights was to have him hold it to my ear so that I could hear the *tick-tick-tick*.

But father was not a man to remain content with managing a small country co-operative. His eyes scanned wider horizons; he looked at the world, like the sage Dr. Johnson, from China to Peru—or perhaps it was from China to Venezuela. (My father, as I mentioned earlier, was unwittingly subject to the contemptuous and derisive nickname—among my female relations—of 'Ven'.) He never travelled far, but, for all that, was more of a traveller than those who have actually viewed the Golden Gate. There was, after all, the nonconformist obsession with money to be reckoned with. If you made money you were, *ipso facto*, a good man, one whom the Presbyterian God had favoured. If not, why, you were little better than an RC (Father Poland excepted) who would do appallingly wicked things, like attending Sunday football matches or go dog racing at Dunmore Park! Thus, there was life on the one hand, the dream on the other: the unending grind at disagreeable chores, and the counter-feeling that race-tracks and whiskey (and, perhaps a bit surreptitiously, slyly, lovely women) were around the corner. Had not other country boys, forsaking plough and spade and hoe, made their way in the big redbrick city and ended up as pot-bellied aldermen who golfed at the weekend with elevated gents such as bank managers, solicitors and doctors?

During father's lifetime I never understood him, nor did he understand me. We lived, for the most part, in a thick fog of non-comprehension. To me he was a darkly-brooding, narrow-jowled, moody man, who, to my disgust, chewed twist tobacco and spat out the liquorice-coloured juice, drank a great deal of noxious-smelling whiskey and believed that a man who had not made a fortune was "no bloody good". He lacked the gift for happiness or enjoyment. My mother and her sisters kept harping on the theme of his addiction to the bottle, and spoke with bated breath of the sinfulness thereof. I did not know so much about the sinful part of it—anything nice seemed always to be a sin—but drinking was obviously something that made a man miserable. Why does he do it, I thought, if he does not find it enjoyable, if it makes him sick? I had yet to hear of Sigmund Freud.

But father being a good Prod in his heart (not that he was a kirk regular) was damned if he would do anything so fiendishly Papist or foreign as enjoy himself! My mother liked fun far more than he did, and delighted in what she called 'droll stories'. She liked innocent amusement, so long as it did not cost too much, for there were bills to pay. Pennies had to be counted—and even half-pennies. In the years when we ran the Kenilworth, we used to get a free cinema pass for displaying showcards of the current films. My mother and I, rigged out in our second-best clothes, would go off together to see films such as *Silent Hour*, which starred her great favourite, the very gentlemanly George Arliss, the very model of an English gentleman. Earlier I had been taken to see *Ramona* by Aunt Tillie in—of all places!—the Clonard, right in the heart of Rome, you might say. The mission bells were indeed calling!

Father came to a film once or twice, but he insisted—much to my chagrin—on leaving in the middle of the big picture saying he could not make head or tail of it. Like most of his relations, he thought the silver screen a lot of high-falutin' nonsense, a veritable fraud perpetrated on decent people—Uncle George considered this wonderful never-never land nothing more than "a wheen o' oul' shadows mugs pay to gape at". Another time, I wheedled Ven into getting as far as the Classic, that palace of romance to my eyes. He hesitated at the box-office, decided against and pressed a half-crown into my sticky palm with the words "Better in your pocket than in some fat oul' showman's". I could have wept. Excitement was what I hungered for, not a coin.

To an uncritical cinema-goer like myself, any and every film was vastly exciting. I could be as happy in the Pop on a Saturday afternoon, watching a western among the scruffy, smelly, jostling, orange-sucking young plebs, as in one of those swish new establishments that impressed me far more than any cathedral had ever done. The Pop may have been rowdy and the noise a bit too much at times to allow one to hear the film dialogue properly, but it had the advantage of costing exactly one penny, merely 'a wing'. Matinees at posh places might cost as much as fourpence or even fivepence. All right for the nobs, but obviously the kind of place I could only visit as a very special treat. As I got a bit older, mere shootin' and killin' and ridin' on the range, with a dramatic chase before the villains were brought to justice, began to seem like kids' stuff.

The sophisticated world began to entrance me. What posh rooms—more like baronial halls than anything else—these high-class Yanks lived in and how they drank their cocktails with poise and charm! With what insouciance the elegant English actor could carry off a situation in which I would have curled up and died with embarrassment! How enviable were these lives that were played out against a Manhattan or Berkeley Square background! Nobody there worried about whether something cost sixpence, unlike the drab, damp, taxi-less, evening-gownless world where one queued for a fish supper (price fivepence) in Joe's steamy saloon near the Pop. I liked grandeur, swank, pretentiousness, no doubt because such attitudes contrasted so violently with the horrible pinching and scraping that went on around me. The world symbolised by revolving doors that led into Grand Hotels of the Vicki Baum/Arnold Bennett type had a glamour far removed from the atmosphere of McMahon's Select Bar or Ross's pawnshop, with its aroma of camphorated clothes.

I was tired of existing. I cried out for life—or what I mistakenly took to be life. Father believed, as I developed into adolescence, that my head had been turned with nonsense I read in the boys' magazines we sold in the shop, and picked up from the gossip columns of the London newspapers. And no doubt it was. Not only that, but I was at the stage where I read any tit-bit I could find about sex, and viewed with delight photos of naked ladies I came across in journals devoted to the cult of nudism. But the world of high-life was only a temporary aberration, and soon I was to become too serious by half, and be filled with zeal for reforming the world. Nudist magazines were to be replaced by intellectual nourishment represented by the *Irish Democrat* (to which paper I contributed my very first article, 'A Youth's Views on Education') and those limp-cover books issued by the Left Book Club. But that time was not yet.

Ven and I were at loggerheads as usual. He denounced me for always having my nose stuck in a book or newspaper or magazine. My eagerness to understand the world around me (not just in a dry, academic way, but in a real human sense) left him cold. Nor did he forgive me for taking naturally to those uppish garments known as pyjamas—'pan-jams' he called them contemptuously—introduced into our household by my Aunt Tillie, whom he loathed and I loved. I knew somehow that the lovely actresses would despise a boy who slept in his shirt, and the approval of ladies was for me far more important than that of Ven. Father still slept in the shirt he wore all day long. His ancestors had done the same thing, assuming they all had shirts to their backs, which I rather doubt. What was good enough for honest men was good enough for Ven. Why wear fancy clothes when you were asleep? The more he sneered the more adamant I became. He complained that my shoes—he wore boots—had pointy toes and that I looked 'a regular show' in my white trousers—these were simply grey worsted pants, though not as wide as I would really have enjoyed having.

Nor did he like the classy, polite way I learned to talk at Methody, using big words, foreign phrases and schoolboy slang in a manner that obviously indicated a 'swelled head' and would never have passed muster anywhere near Cootehill. I began to be grammatical and say 'he's gone' instead of 'he's went', which showed that college affectation had insidiously crept in. Worse still, I began to pronounce English in a slightly anglicised way. That was also wrong. The more critical Ven became the more determined I was to make myself as different from him as I could, especially since these new directions had the warm approval of Aunt Tillie, who wanted me to be a gentleman like the McCreas, whom she said were "all doctors and clergy".

There was daily evidence of his dislike for me and his feeling that, fundamentally, I sided with the feminine McCrea establishment, with its good humour, snobbery, conformity, hard work and relish in innocent amusement. Yet, at times, during a troubled boyhood—dark and haunted, yet not without an innate belief that one day I would live the life of Larry, far, far away from the Newtownards Road—a temporary bond would spring up between us, as it did in earlier days when I sat on his knee and combed his dark, grey-flecked hair. In the long, timeless evenings of July and August, I would take the beloved football I had obtained by collecting a set of cards from a boys' paper and off the two of us would go for a tram-ride that brought us to a destination such as Bellevue or Glengormley. We would hurtle through the still evening air, surveying the now inactive city from the top of, no, not a tram—a red chariot rocking its way ever onwards, that thrilled and pulsated with the energy of some elemental force. Those tram-rides were pure ecstasy. It was the route homeward that I feared, when he called at pub after pub for "just a wee minute". With tears in my eyes, we would come back to the shop, eyed by disapproving or amused neighbours.

Ven once went for about a week into a nursing home off the Lisburn Road, an institution that specialised in the treatment of nervous diseases. There he had electric shock treatment. I went to see him there and, for the first time in my life, played table tennis, that very genteel middle-class game. Within a few weeks of coming out he was, in my mother's words, "at it again. Paralytic!" When she uttered words like these, she would first raise her eyes to heaven and begin to snivel, drying her eyes with her apron. I would go hot and cold, feeling a little angry, very afraid and thoroughly ashamed. Then would come the scenes that occurred regularly and made me as tense as an old maid who wakes up to find a man under the bed.

During these theatrical interludes, Ven would rant obscenities at mother or even strike her, or, in a tantrum, throw his food into the fire, or threaten to beat me "within an inch of my life", or assert that mother and her relations had dissipated the fortune that he had made, and that he would have the law on the McCrea villains and leave them penniless. All these and more threats came out of an abysmally deep reservoir of alcoholic aggression, despair and self-pity. "They ruined me, the McCreas have ruined me," he would inform people who could not care less. Shaw remarked that home is the girl's prison and the woman's workhouse. It was certainly a workhouse for mother. 'Home Sweet Home' seemed an ironic phrase, or else one coined by people out of touch with reality. It was a place I was always glad to leave, and to which I returned with some misgiving. It was sour-smelling and affectionless. Fortunately, from time to time, I retreated to Aunt Tillie's where the atmosphere was always warm and cheerful, only shadowed by Ven's latest misdeed.

Home was where one slept and little more than that. Schoolmasters at least dispensed a rough justice. They could be respected, or most of them could. Their punishment was seldom unduly severe and seldom undeserved, whereas Ven was arbitrary and one never knew what might happen if he lost his temper. Like some of our politicians, he exercised power without responsibility. Authority—Ven's excepted—was not too bad, and after the first rebellion of youth and early manhood, authority in its various forms is something with which I have had little difficulty in coming to terms. Not for me the lifelong urge to be 'agin the government'. Coming from a household where civil war and alarms of one kind and another were to be expected, I came early to believe in Henry Miller's dictum: "Peace, it's wonderful!"

Not that I was altogether a peace-at-any-price or *danegeld* boy in the incessant war against Ven, which was sometimes cold, sometimes hot. As in all wars, there came a crisis, a turning-point. It happened one summer day in 1935, when I was not quite fifteen. I had been out in the back yard, breaking up into sticks a number of wooden boxes in which goods had been delivered to the shop. This was something Ven used to order me to do when he was a bit high. I resented his manner of ordering it to be done, and the way his pale, dissatisfied face would press to the window to see the job was being carried out to his satisfaction. As a matter of fact, I rather enjoyed the task in itself, and I liked to do it well, always having had an instinctive desire to excel. It was, as I recall, a warm August afternoon, and soon I had broken up all the boxes. A little out of breath from the hurried exertion, I brushed up the wood chips and put them in the bin. I threw down the hatchet with satisfaction after a job well done. I was pleased with myself and hoped now to sneak past the old man and into the shop to ask mother's permission to go and visit Billy Davidson, a school pal who lived in the Malone Road end of town. This boy's father was a box manufacturer—I was a little flattered that a boy whose family actually had a skivvy found me interesting, and Aunt Tillie encouraged me to get to know such people. I had my way to make in the world, she said, and influential friends would be all to the good. Then an ugly face appeared at the window, glaring at me with bloodshot eyes. Speak of the devil—if it wasn't the 'oul' lad', and in a bit of a paddy, too! What eyes! Had he escaped from Purdysburn or what? Out he rushed like a bull stung by a wasp.

"I didn't tell you to stop," he screamed. "You fucking idiot!"

"I won't do any more. I've finished the job in any case. And I've got a friend to see."

"You're a bloody idiot—you an' yer fancy white trousers, an' yer grand college chums. A lot of oul' cissies."

"And you're drunk,' I retorted. "You're talking through your headgear."

"Drunk, you impudent pup," he screamed, "I'll show you who's drunk, you fucking half-blind get. You don't even know who your da is. He's down at the market sellin' oranges. Ask that oul' whore in the shop."

"I'll kill him," I thought, "I'll kill him if he lays a finger on me, so help me God."

He had struck me in the past—and I was afraid he might smash my nice new glasses into my eyes and blind me. As it was, it was no fun being short sighted, and it handicapped me badly at games. Words would get me precisely nowhere. Action now or never! I picked up the hatchet and lingeringly touched its slightly jagged gleaming edge with my left forefinger. I was a-tremble with fear and anger. Then I spoke, slowly, deliberately.

"Get inside, you dirty lying drunkard or I'll cut you open," adding for good measure, "Whiskey Ven."

He opened his mouth to say something nasty, but, drunk as he was, he read the word that shone behind my lenses. The word was 'murder'. This was no play-acting and he knew it. Muttering incoherently, he turned, groped his way into the kitchen, and slithered into the swivel office chair. In a moment, he fell off it on to the worn linoleum.

Feeling ashamed and angry, I rushed into the house and out through the shop, not stopping to answer my mother's question as to where I was going. I ran wildly into the street, then turned left and ran. Past Kenilworth Street, past Fraser Street, past Cable Street, on and on, past Maidment's the greengrocers, on towards Connswater and the Holywood Arches. I glanced over at the Northern Bank where I carried the shop's weekly takings every Saturday morning. I carried my hundred pounds or more with dignity. Look at me now, a fugitive from Ven! The sun seemed to burn down as if to impede the progress of a malefactor. Old wives' tales came to mind. Had not Aunt Tillie once told me of the little boy who struck his parents, and how he died soon after of a brainstorm, and how even to this very day his fleshless hand stuck up out of his little grave. Oh yes, you had to 'Honour Thy Father and Thy Mother ...' Yet how could one give honour where it was obviously unwarranted? Surely God was a just God? Nobody I knew could be asked to solve the dilemma, neither minister nor Sunday school teacher, for this was something which must, at all costs, be kept secret.

I kept on and on, past grocers' shops and newsagents and pubs and butchers' shops and pawnbrokers and police barracks, until at last I came to sedate houses along the route to Holywood. I stopped running, for the chances were now less that a peeler would stop me and ask me to explain myself. How could a Methody boy explain that he had wanted to kill his father? It was inexcusable and would appal one of these dark-suited pillars of law and order. Or supposing the headmaster in College Gardens heard of this hou-ha? Supposing Ven went to the head to complain about insubordination—heaven knows, he had often threatened to go up to the school and disgrace me in front of my fine new friends. If I were expelled, what would become of me without having passed Junior or Senior? A life as a caulker in the yard. Goodbye to my hopes of being a big man in London. London would callously close its gates to such a boy. These were my thoughts as I wandered, shirt sticking to my back, towards Holywood and the sea ... Now in the open country, I climbed through a hedge and into a field. I wept bitterly for having wanted to kill Ven, for, despite everything, he was my father. "God forgive me," I prayed fervently. And I repeated the Lord's Prayer with a sincerity very different from the way I gabbled it normally before jumping into bed.

It was chilly when I returned, sneaking past the New Princess cinema, whose second house was just being let out. Tired and hungry and dishevelled I certainly was, but I felt strangely radiant and unafraid. I had purged my crime. Not only that, but at last I had done something. I had stood up for myself and would now take what consequences came my way. The shop was shut of course when I arrived, so I rattled the letter-box with as much confidence as I could summon up. My mother came to the door. Her eyes were red, and she looked much older than usual. I noticed the grey in her hair.

"Where were you, boy?" she asked. Her relief seemed to have an undertone of anger, a controlled anger, unlike Ven's.

"Out with a friend. Billy Davidson. We went to Holywood."

"You look as if you'd been through a hedge backwards. Why didn't you say where you were going instead of rushing out like a mad thing? I was worried to death about you, Robbie. First your father, now you ... The Greacens are all mad! I never saw the like of them, not like my people ..."

"You should've known I'd be all right, mother. Honestly I was. I wish you wouldn't treat me like a child. I wanted to get away from Ven, if you must know."

She began to weep into her apron, a sight that always made me feel guilty, but I was powerless to do or say anything. Something in me wanted to comfort her, but I could not or would not. What did I care about this crazy world of grown-ups with their tears and anger and admonitions, don't-do-this and don't-do-that! When I grew up, I'd be off and I'd never come back. Never, never!

I went into the scullery, poured out a cup of buttermilk and made myself a big piece. I ate hurriedly, standing. Without a goodnight to mother, I ran up the creaking stairs to the attic room where I slept. I didn't know if Ven had gone to bed or was still out, nor did I care. Then I lit my candle with a Swift match— we had no electric light at the top of the house—and got into bed. I lay for a long time watching the shadows. Opening *Vanity Fair* I tried to read, but could not settle to it. Tomorrow was a new day, I thought. Perhaps I could re-learn to honour Ven as I should. Perhaps not. It did not seem to matter much. Only a few more years and I would be out of the prison house, free to do as I pleased. I put out the candle and felt the darkness swathe me like a cloak—friendly and comforting.

About a week later, I was coming home from having had tea at the house of a schoolfriend, for I was making every effort to cultivate the right people. Some book I had been reading stressed the need for contacts. I had every intention of making my way in the world and I had a contempt for those without ambition. For my part, I would have a shot at getting the best that was going. The idea of one man being as good as another—dear to many an average Ulster heart—was loathsome. I considered I was superior to most, and I wanted them to know it, too. Yet I sensed that that attitude caused resentment, even bitterness. Well, let it! I vowed that one day my achievements would outstrip those of the boys brought up on the Malone Road. In the past week, things had taken a turn for the better in the place I called home. Ven had been off the booze for three whole days!

At the corner of Templemore Avenue, I saw a group of people surrounding a navy-suited figure that seemed to have slipped into the roadway. A brown felt hat lay forlornly on the ground. As I approached I saw a man, red-faced and beefy like a cattle-dealer, holding in his clumsy hands a tradesman's bicycle with a big wicker basket above a low wheel. There was a sign under the bar that read, 'Cochrane: Flesher of Quality'. I heard the big man's shrill, angry voice splutter out: "If drunken eejits get in my road it isn't my fault if I run them down."

A weak voice from the ground: "You ... you ... I'll ... law on you."

I came closer. Through my well-polished, steel-rimmed new glasses I realised with a shudder that the figure in the roadway was Ven. I thought of my mother's words—"May Ven never come home alive this day!"—and how nearly they had come true.

I burned with anger and shame that I should be the son of such a man. How God had punished me and how I hated Him! But my anger found an earthly target—it flared up against the red-faced oaf who held the bicycle in his rough hands like a mother grasping her only babe—as if his wretched tradesman's bicycle were studded with diamonds! Summoning up my every bit of courage, I pushed my way through the gawking bystanders.

"Look here, mister," I said, "clear off to hell, you fucking baboon. He's my *father*."

Still burning with rage and shame, I pulled Ven from the gutter, shoved the brown felt hat on his head and dragged him home. When we got in, mother started a tirade against drunkenness.

"Shut up, woman," I said roughly.

Then I ran hell for leather up the stairs to my little room, where I fell sobbing on the hard but familiar bed. It seemed to me as if I had been crying on and off for hours before I at last came to my senses, and decided to have a wash. I carefully brushed and combed my auburn locks, looking at myself appraisingly in the cracked mirror. I had pushed all thought of Ven out of my mind, and was dreaming instead of the golden world I should enter in the distant future and in some distant place. The world of famous men and beautiful women beckoned to me ... and I knew they were all waiting ... waiting for Robert.

TEN

Not An Inch

Uncle George down in County Monaghan hardly ever wrote a letter. One day, however, we heard from him. He had a request. Could we board the son of a neighbouring farmer for a weekly sum? Uncle George assured us that the young man's family was most respectable and Orange to the core. I remembered having met this young man on one of my visits, though my memory of him had blurred. Mother was dubious about the idea, though she admitted we could do with the money. Where would he sleep? Father had a prompt reply: "With your son, of course."

This way he had of referring to me as my mother's son both irritated and pleased me, for implicit in it was a denial of his paternity. I cared not a straw whether I was his son. I was willing to settle for a father who might be more to my liking than the one I was saddled with. Father had sometimes said that my real father sold oranges at the market. I would answer, "Why not? A lot better than being a candidate for an inebriate's home, isn't it?"

This stung father as I intended. Mother hated this bitter exchange between us and would say sharply to me, "Now that's quite enough. You know I don't like that kind of talk". Anyway, several days passed while the pros and cons of taking in a boarder were weighed up. At last, it was decided that Tommy Gibson— that being the potential boarder's name—would be accepted. After all, if he proved troublesome he could be got rid of.

I had mixed feelings about the arrival of a boarder. This Gibson fellow was some six or seven years older than me. My memory of him began to clear. On the occasions when we had met in the country, I had not particularly liked him. I sensed that he considered me the sort of townee who had little enthusiasm for fishing or shooting. On the other hand, I had not found Gibson positively objectionable or I would have made my views clear when he was being discussed. I suffered a bit from loneliness as an only child, so that the idea of sharing my bedroom with someone had a certain amount to be said for it. His modest financial contribution every week would be of help in our finances and I could put up a plea for more pocket money. I needed more and more money for the second-hand books I was beginning to buy. Therefore I adopted a wait-and-see, neutral attitude to the plan to import a stranger.

Tommy Gibson turned out to be a presentable, not too countrified, fresh-complexioned young man in his early twenties. His eyes were grey and keen. He was of average height and stood erect, a trifle stiffly. Under a surface politeness, he had a challenging aspect. He talked about the need to preserve law and order, and keep dissidents in their place. Of his father he said: "He's like yours—not worth a damn." He had a commendable frankness. Tommy Gibson had started looking to the right in politics, a redneck in search of a leader. I looked to the left.

By twenty-three or so, Tommy had tried several careers. He had nothing in the way of school certificates, not, indeed, that he was stupid in any usual sense. He had often mitched from school and had left as soon as he could. Brought up among the stony small fields and lakes of Monaghan, he had handled rod and rifle since he was little more than a child. He was a hunter. On a visit to County Monaghan, I mentioned Tommy's name to an arthritic old man who remembered him: "That Tommy Gibson could kill anything that moved—a real shot that same boy. I mind him as a wee lad comin' back at dusk wet to the skin and carryin' over his shoulder the biggest salmon you ever did see. Divil the keeper could catch that wee lad." Tommy, I gathered, hunted alone. He wanted nobody's help or sympathy. So far he had been a lorry driver—for he had useful hands with machines—a farmer's boy and a garage mechanic in Dundalk. None of these jobs satisfied him. Besides, he had no liking for what we called 'the Free State'. Nor for freedom.

Tommy was a very neat fellow and could put his finger on all his possessions instantly. He imposed law and order on them. We got on reasonably well, although he annoyed me once by pointing a contemptuous finger at my books and saying: "A lot of nonsense all that stuff. Where do you think that'll get you, boy? What do you want fillin' your head with soft drivel?"

"Books interest me," I replied priggishly. "I can learn from them. That's why."

Tommy laughed sneeringly. I blushed and stayed silent. We would not become friends.

I never learned exactly where Tommy Gibson went every morning with his shining, carefully shaved face, in his tidy brown suit, stiff white collar and highly polished shoes. He had some vague temporary job.

I suspected he was up to something on the quiet, for he seemed never to be short of money. He wore a smart hat with a feather and the brim tilted at an angle detectives affected in Hollywood films. I sensed that Tommy had a secret ambition he preferred to keep to himself. Certainly he would not confide in a youngster like me, especially one not of his own *macho* kind.

Tommy was out most evenings. He once said something about drilling, for I knew he was a member of the B-Specials. He sometimes did physical jerks in the bedroom. One evening, my curiosity overcame my scruples. I knew Tommy had a cardboard folder containing photos, letters and documents, since I once saw him placing a letter in the folder as I came into the bedroom unexpectedly. He then asked me to fetch him a glass of water and when I returned with it the folder was out of sight.

It was far from being a practice of mine to sneak a look at anybody's private papers but, for once, the temptation was too

100

great to resist. It would alleviate boredom, the feeling of flatness I often had in the period when I returned from school and before we had evening supper. I washed my hands carefully before the operation lest I should make the slightest mark, for Tommy had hawk-like eyes. A quick search put me right on target. The third drawer I opened contained the buff folder, an edge of which was exposed under a newspaper. I took it out as if it were an original Shakespeare Folio, noting the word 'Private' written in red ink in Tommy's childish calligraphy.

Opening the folder, I came on an assortment of photos of relatives and girlfriends, handwritten letters and programmes of sports meetings. I nearly closed it without reading anything, for I had a sense of shame about what I was doing. Then I saw an official-looking envelope. Tempted, I decided to read the letter presumably inside the envelope and then call it a day. After all, Tommy might sneak up the stairs in those polished shoes of his, or mother might come up for some reason and surprise me in the act of reading our lodger's correspondence. If she did, I would never hear the end of it.

Soon I was reading the letter that had attracted me. It was a reply to Tommy's application to join the police, the Royal Ulster Constabulary. The RUC was a body of men—each of them armed—highly esteemed by Protestants and disliked, even hated, by nationalists and republicans. The letter referred to a recent interview and pointed out regretfully that Tommy, although highly suitable in every other respect, was below the minimum height for entry.

Had he been merely half-an-inch below the required height, something might have been done because of his excellent record as a B-Special. As it was, they regretted ... I was reminded immediately of the local political slogan—Not an Inch! Then I heard an urgent voice calling: "Robbie, I want you to run a message for me." The buff folder was hurriedly put away and I ran down the stairs to see what mother wanted done. I forgot all about Tommy Gibson's ambition to be a policeman.

That night I slept soundly, as one always does when one has

penetrated the secret of another. I had congratulated myself on my enterprise and cleverness. In the morning, I had just finished dressing when Tommy, an early riser, came into the room. He was frowning.

"Have you a headache?" I asked, trying to look innocent.

"Now look here, boy," he answered. "I'm going to ask you a question and I don't want a lie."

I winced at the contempt in the word 'boy', but bit my lip. I did not at all like the rasp in Tommy's voice.

"How often have you been through my correspondence?"

"I don't know what you're talking about," I stammered.

"You're a liar and a son of a drunken liar," Tommy replied coolly. "You damned well know what I'm talking about, you wee get."

He opened the drawer I myself had opened and brought out the buff folder.

"Have you seen this before?" he asked.

"No," I said. He flushed.

"You bloody liar," he said. "You're only making things worse for yourself. How dare you read my letters, you impudent bastard."

I kept quiet. Lies had failed. There was punishment on the way and I had got to take it. Not a whimper, that was it, no matter what happened. "In future," said Tommy, "when you read someone's letters you should at least take care not to put them back *upside down*! They don't teach you much that's useful at that fine college, do they? I'm warning you that if you ever put a finger on anything of mine again, I'll break the glasses into your eyes. I'll bloody well blind you."

He pulled the glasses off my face and threw them on the table. Then he struck me violently across the face so I could feel the hard metal of his ring cutting into my nose. Had he broken it? I made no attempt to defend myself.

"You impudent bastard," he repeated. "Get out of here before I really start work on you."

Blood streamed down my face. Some blobs of blood had got

on to my collar and school tie. Fortunately, I got out of the house without being seen by mother. I went to Matron at school and explained I had fallen off my bike. She cleaned up the mess.

Tommy stayed with us for another two months or so. Never a word was spoken of our little scene. Mother accepted my explanation and told me I must be more careful on the bike or one day I would be killed. Father contented himself with the remark that I looked a proper eejit. I let it pass for I had enough of a wound for the time being.

Tommy, I discovered, was one of those who took delight in handing out punishment. He told me with satisfaction of how he had interrogated an IRA suspect. He took this man off to a lonely wood, having told his fellow B-Specials he wanted to talk to the man privately. He beat him up in a way that the man would have no visible scars in case a Nationalist MP tried to take the matter up. "The police are too bloody soft," said Tommy. "I made the bugger talk."

"What did you do?" I asked.

"Do you think I'd tell a nosey bugger like you?" answered Tommy.

Occasionally I went out with Tommy. I knew he despised me but, now that I had taken my punishment well, his contempt had somewhat diminished. I liked to watch him in action. Even when he was wearing plain clothes he stopped the traffic like a real policeman. People obeyed him sheepishly. To corner louts he would say "Move on!"—and they would do so! Anyone other than Tommy would have been in for trouble. An open razor might have been flashed. But Tommy had an air of authority that all recognised.

Thwarted in his aim of becoming a policeman and bored by civilian life, Tommy joined the RAF. We heard that he was driving petrol lorries. How frustrated he must have been waiting for the war to begin. On the day he left Belfast for training, I helped him take his luggage to the Great Northern station. We shook hands without cordiality. Although younger, I was quite a bit taller than Tommy. I could not resist the comment, "Height isn't everything". He smiled sourly and, as the train moved out, said, not unkindly, "Nosey bugger".

I never saw Tommy Gibson again. In 1942, news came that he had been killed in an accident in England.

Shortly after the end of the war, I found myself in a carriage of the Liverpool-London boat train with a fellow Belfastman. He was a chatty, pleasant fellow who began to reminisce about his days in the RAF.

"Them was the days and no mistake," he said, sighing and lighting a cigarette.

I discovered he had joined up about the same time as Tommy, and in Belfast, so I asked if by any chance he had come across Tommy.

"Don't say you knew that bastard," he replied. "I'll never forget him."

"I didn't know him all that well," I said.

"Lucky you," said the Belfastman. "Do you know that he once broke an aircraftsman's thumb for cheeking him?"

"I heard he was killed in an accident," I said.

"Some accident," said my companion with a smile.

"What happened?" I enquired.

"Well, I don't know all the details, but the long and short of it is that Tommy's lorry blew up somewhere near Wolverhampton. They called it an accident, but the boys wanted to get their own back. Mind you, he got a great funeral. Flowers and drums and all that. Yes, Tommy Gibson got a splendid military funeral."

He winked and lit another cigarette. Perhaps it was only my imagination but there seemed something odd about the man's right hand thumb.

ELEVEN

A Gentle Man

"As dacent a man as ever stepped in leather shoes," said the man from Corrigan's garage in Castleblayney as he drove me out to Grigg. He referred to my Uncle George who had a farm adjoining that of Aunt Liz-Ann, with whom I would be staying. Uncle George's land was mainly meadow and my aunt's hilly, her house perched at the top of a steep lane. These summer visits were a delight both in reality and in anticipation.

According to the amount of my luggage and how much money I had in my pocket, I would either walk the three or four miles out to Grigg or travel in comfort. The long climb up the narrow lane was not altogether to the liking of a city boy, especially in the dark, for I always remember arriving at Castleblayney station just as night was closing in. I slightly feared the darkness of this alien landscape, where bushes could look menacing. Crime in those days was minimal and it was not fear of being robbed that worried me, but fear that I might be set upon for not belonging to the right tribe. Yet, as the years passed, my fears grew less and less. It was odd that the Catholics of Belfast were enemies and those of Monaghan were friends.

Father spoiled it all for me by saying that my Aunt Liz-Ann had told him I was a nuisance and only kept her back from farm work. During my last two or three years at school, I would not go back despite repeated invitations. Then, when I was perhaps about twenty-four or twenty-five, I paid a final visit. It was the last time I would see my aunt and uncle who had been so kind to me as a child and young boy

On that occasion, I had a feeling of awkwardness. The distances had shrunk, her farmhouse seemed smaller than I remembered it, the collie dog's welcoming bark less resonant. Nor did I come alone. Patricia, my wife-to-be, came with me. I wanted her to meet some of my relatives. She made an immediate rapport with them.

Aunt Liz-Ann, as I recall her, was a little woman, a little stooped but active as the day was long, busy with chickens and calves and pigs to be fed, occupied with milking and churning and baking and cooking. It was only years later that I realised how much work had to be done on a small farm for relatively meagre returns. Like most of my relatives, she had no time to be neurotic or wonder whether or not she was happy.

Aunt Liz-Ann had been left a widow with one child, a daughter, Sadie, who was perhaps eighteen months older than me. Most of the time, Sadie and I got on well and I enjoyed meeting her friends, some of them fellow-pupils at Dundalk Grammar School to which Sadie commuted daily. She cycled in to Castleblayney and caught the train there. The journey to and from school must not have been enticing in the depths of winter, but country folk were hardy and thought nothing of being soaked to the skin or wretchedly cold. We street-wise townees had our own kind of toughness, but traipsing up and down muddy lanes was not one of them. We would not shirk a fight, but a lengthy walk did not appeal to us if we could ride in a tramcar.

Uncle George towered above his sister (in fact, his half-sister) Liz-Ann. Much later, I wrote a poem about him:

Sometimes he'd grip my hand
In his rough bulbous gentle fist,
Then guide me over fence and *sheugh*.
I'd watch him out of big child eyes
Half hope to see the beast run free.

106

I'd hear the whole townland explode,
The chuckle at his hunter's skill.
Guns, harrows, ploughs his holy artefacts,
His pulpit was his workshop,
Toil his route to paradise.
Sunday saw him dressed in navy serge
Edwardian cut as in his youth,
Knife creases made by mattress weight.
In Bible mood he'd hold his peace
Huddle close to the turf fire
Wrestle with John Knox's God.
He prophesied I'd live to see
The sun turn black at noon,
Earthquakes, meadows red with blood.
Each March I call to mind
His orchard massed with daffodils,
Their dance of life, their dance of death.

He liked to play practical jokes and these could frighten me, as when one night he wailed like a banshee before jumping out from behind a hedge. His images were simple, many of his phrases *clichés*—food and drink went "down the red lane"; before leaving a house he would say he had "to make tracks". Interested in the supernatural though he was, I doubt whether he really believed in ghosts. Protestants usually did not and maintained that Catholics did. Certainly, though, he would not cut down a fairy thorn as that would bring bad luck.

Uncle George had a house of his own, thickly carpeted by dust and spartanly furnished. Here he sometimes slept but mainly he ate and bedded in his sister's well-swept house on the hill. From time to time, he would hole up in his bachelor establishment for days on end when the mood took him. No one knew why. Perhaps he had taken offence for some reason and was sulking. He belonged to that breed of northerner known as 'dour', so that he could sit in silence for long periods as if the world around him did not exist. Then his face would brighten and he would tell a story about some local event, a wake or a wedding. These wakes and weddings, I noticed, always took place among the Catholic community. Protestants did not celebrate anything except the Twelfth of July. Many of them were teetotallers and nonsmokers and frowned on entertainment of any kind. They would no more play football on a Sunday than a Jew would eat pork. Yet when a few Protestants met together they could be jovial enough, even without alcohol. Cleanliness, tidiness, making money honestly—these were Protestant ideals.

Now, if Uncle George associated more with Catholic neighbours than others in the family, it was not because of any tendency towards their theology or liturgy. Like all of us, he had a strong suspicion of anything that came under the heading of Popery, which was considered a perversion of Christian truth as found in the Old and New Testaments. I have the impression that, in those days, too much emphasis was placed on the Old Testament and the idea of a God of Wrath, rather than on the tolerance and forgiveness taught by Christ. Typically puritanical, Uncle George neither smoked nor drank alcohol, and I never heard him swear. He was, so far as I could find out, a total abstainer from wine, Woodbines and women.

Others in the family regarded Uncle George with amused tolerance. He worked hard, yet his enterprise bore little fruit. He was more indifferent to money than most Protestants, who tended to believe that a God-fearing life would bring prosperity. He was content to have a dry bed—two, in fact, one in his own house and one in Liz-Ann's—and to eat home-cured salty bacon, floury potatoes sauced by butter, scones and soda farls and potato bread, and to drink copious draughts of buttermilk and tea. Oh, I nearly forgot to mention porridge, which was eaten both for breakfast and last thing at night before going to bed. Uncle George could not see why a man wanted whiskey and stout or fancy cuisine if he had on his table good country fare. He may well have been right and the city slickers wrong.

Uncle George once became angry with me for pointing a gun at the collie. The dog cringed under the table, moaning piteously.

"Never," said Uncle George sternly, "never let me see you do that again. Never point a gun at a person or a dog. It might be loaded."

Another memory of a summer visit drawing to an end. The days had stretched into weeks. I had experimented with smoking and had lain under a tree watching the blue smoke curl upwards but then had a fit of coughing. It was a fruitful and lucky experiment that put me off smoking for life, all the more odd in that both my parents' and aunts' shops sold cigarettes and I could easily have helped myself to them. I used to go for cycle runs here and there, and occasionally meet other young people but, for the most part, I was content enough to loaf around or occasionally give a hand with the farm work. I hesitated to offer my services—not out of laziness, but because I feared that a townee would not do whatever job it was properly. But now field and lane and barn and orchard would soon be abandoned for the red trams of Belfast and the classrooms that smelled of chalk and polished wood and disinfectant. Heaven had lain about me for six weeks and I had buried myself in *Lorna Doone* and *Wuthering Heights.*

Uncle George got the trap ready and harnessed Bessie, the mare he loved more than many men love their wives. There seemed to be all the time in the world and I was in no haste for the end of the idyll. I wallowed in the sweet melancholy of adolescence and Uncle George was as calm as a lake surface on a windless day. I kissed Aunt Liz-Ann and cousin Sadie goodbye and off we went down the loanen. Soon we were trotting along the main road past Johnny McQuade's farm and heading for the station in Castleblayney.

Everything was going as harmoniously as a marriage bell until we met a neighbour coming in the opposite direction. This was a sour, grumpy man called Foxy Adair, a Protestant as it happened, a man somewhat unpopular in the district. Uncle George stopped to say hello and mentioned the train I wanted to catch.

"Well now," said Foxy with an air of satisfaction, "the wee lad won't get on that train unless that mare of yours grows wings."

109

He put the enormous gold watch back in his pocket having delivered his bad news. Foxy Adair smiled knowingly.

Uncle George immediately took command of the situation as if he were the Iron Duke reincarnated and faced with a problem at Waterloo. He turned to me and said, "Don't worry. You'll catch that train or my name isn't George Greacen."

Bessie seemed to understand what had happened for she lifted her dainty hooves and ran as if she were going to meet her favourite stallion. Melancholy gave way to excitement. I wanted to prove old Foxy wrong, Uncle George wanted to prove him wrong—and so did Bessie. Just as we got to the bridge we heard the hiss of steam—there she came! Uncle George betrayed no emotion but simply urged Bessie to a final spurt. In we went to the station yard.

I jumped down, and ran with my ticket in hand as if it were a passport to the Garden of Eden. Within seconds, I had got into the train just as the whistle was blown and the train started to move. I saw Uncle George come lurching in with my suitcase, but by now the train was gathering speed. I waved to him and shouted, "We've beaten old Foxy—thanks to you and Bessie".

Victory was ours and it was sweet. What did it matter about the battered old cardboard suitcase?

TWELVE

A Gun in the Corner

Father's brother, my Uncle Robert, lived near Omagh in County Tyrone. He ran what was called a 'model farm' on the latest scientific lines as might be expected from the brains of the family. He also worked as an inspector in the Department of Agriculture and his duties seemed largely to consist of going round the countryside advising farmers on grass management and milk production. Uncle Robert, wholly self-taught, was the only reader in the family. He read not only everything he could find dealing with his own special interests, but also books considered advanced at the time. He was the first man I heard use the word 'psychology'. I once heard him commend the verse of Ella Wheeler Wilcox and there was a book in my parents' house—*In Tune with the Infinite*—that had probably been a gift from Uncle Robert. He was, in fact, the kind of man who, in later times, would have had a brilliant university career.

His work brought him into contact with varied people in the farming community, some of whom valued his expertise and others thought of him as being cranky. On a visit once to Uncle Robert's farm, I was to meet one of his neighbours, an acquaintance named William James Craig. Willie James, as everyone called him, was a bachelor in his early fifties, a thick-set man with legs like tree trunks, large, weather-reddened hands and hair the colour of a herring. He had decided political views for he was known as the staunchest Orangeman in the area. So vehement were his views that he refused all contact with his Catholic neighbours. He neither smoked nor drank. Willie James was respected by Protestants, though few of them really liked him.

One day Uncle Robert took me to Willie James' farmhouse where he was delivering some medicine for a sick calf. This was not, strictly speaking, part of his work but he was a kindly man always prepared to help a neighbour. He did not share Willie John's narrow attitude, but that was neither here nor there when it came to giving assistance. Uncle Robert was frequently called upon to doctor animals and some farmers would swear—assuming a good Protestant *would* swear—that he knew more about how to treat sick animals than most vets.

Willie James kept his house scrupulously clean and tidy. This too appealed to the Protestant mind, with its insistence that cleanliness was next to godliness. Everything in Willie James' place was just so.

What seemed odd was that this big heavy man should be so dainty, even so old-maidish, in his ways.

"So this is your nephew Robbie," said Willie James. "He looks a right wee lad."

I didn't altogether relish the informal 'Robbie' instead of Robert. My uncle was sometimes known as 'Old Robert' and I as 'Young Robert'.

The two men exchanged talk about animals, and presently left me in the kitchen while they went out to tend to the sick calf. I looked round with interest. It was a dull kitchen despite its gleaming oil lamp, the immaculate American cloth on the table, the clasp Bible on the window ledge and the well-scrubbed tiles. Then I saw the gun. It was standing in the corner.

This gun was different from others I had seen—shotguns that were used by the man of the house to shoot rabbits or rats or crows. This was a sturdy and short-barrelled job with a heavy wooden stock. I went over and picked it up, for it was unlikely it would be loaded. I handled it gingerly, remembering Uncle George's rebuke when I pointed a gun at the collie. I tried to

112

read, but could not, what looked like an ornate script engraved on the barrel.

At that very moment the door opened. Willie James scuttled over, snatched the gun out of my hands and put it in the corner.

"That gun's not to be touched by nobody but myself," he said peevishly.

"I'm sure the lad didn't mean any harm," said Uncle Robert, giving me a disapproving look.

"Maybe not," said Willie James doubtfully. "So we'll forget it and hope it won't happen again. What about a wee sup o' tay?"

Willie James bustled about like a housewife, though his movements could hardly be called graceful. Then he turned to me and said, not unkindly, "Robbie, would you be interested in knowing why I'm so particular about that gun? It's a rare one, I can tell you."

"Yes, I would, Mr. Craig."

"Alright then. It'll be something you'll remember all your life."

We sat down at the table—on which our host had placed a new-looking linen tablecloth—to cups of sweet strong tea and soda bread farls. Perhaps Willie James had baked them himself! He began his tale with a question.

"Have you ever heard of Col. Fred Crawford?"

"I don't think so," I replied.

Willie James turned to my uncle. "Dear me, now, do they teach them anything at all in them schools in Belfast?"

The question remained unanswered.

"Well, I dare say you've heard of the UVF."

I nodded and said haltingly, "Ulster Volunteer Force".

"Right you are first time," said Willie James with approval. "That lot of fellas was the heart of corn, so they were. None of your riff-raff or corner boys. I was right proud to be one of them. The UVF took a solemn oath that they would never let the Shinners seize the north without a bloody struggle. An' if the English wanted to sell us out, which I wouldn't put past them, we'd take them on as well."

113

He paused and then went on, "Now you know you can't fight without guns, so what did Col. Fred do but go over to Germany a wheen o' months afore the big war started in August 1914 and bring back thirty thousand o' them wee lads."

He pointed to the rifle in the corner in case we failed to take the drift.

"I don't suppose you know the name of the ship that carried them into Larne. Maybe even your clever uncle doesn't know or has forgotten."

"Indeed, I know the name as well as I know my own," said Uncle Robert. "It was the *Clyde Valley*, wasn't it?"

"The nail has been struck squarely on the head," said Willie James. "This same *Clyde Valley* was the greatest wee ship that ever sailed in salt water. For twenty long years she had been carrying coals over from Lancashire. Now, of course, Col. Fred loaded the guns first of all into the *S.S. Fanny*, another great wee ship, and got away from Hamburg without a paper to his name under cover of fog. The Royal Navy no less was after him but he gave them the slip and got as far as a sea loch in the Hebrides."

Willie was beginning to sweat with excitement. He wiped his brow and went on, "There he left the guns and the ammunition, and off he went to Glasgow where he met a good Unionist fella, a Belfastman who owned the *Clyde Valley*. Within hours the *Clyde Valley* had a Glasgow registration number and was under Col. Fred's control. Next the bold Colonel sent a radio message to the *Fanny* to meet him off the Tuskar Rock."

Willie John paused again to wipe his brow. Then he took up the story again.

"The name *Clyde Valley* was changed for the day to *Mountjoy II*. Then, off the Tuskar Rock the two wee boats were tied together and off they moved quiet as you please, having fixed the navigating lights to make them look like one big fat boat. They hirpled though the water towards Larne, and all night long the work went on."

"What work?" I enquired.

"Are you listenin' at all?" asked Willie James in exasperation.

"Can't you see that they had to transfer the guns—wrapped in bundles of five in oilcloth—from the *Fanny* to her sister ship? When they finished the job, what happened then?"

Neither Uncle Robert nor I could answer that one.

"I'll have to tell you then," said Willie John, after a somewhat dramatic interval.

"They untied the *Fanny* and back to Scotland she went as fast as she could skip. The Royal Navy was searching for her and now, as you might say, she was searching for the Royal Navy. A few hours later she was intercepted by a Royal Navy corvette. Them Navy lads had the surprise of their lives, for not a single gun nor round of ammunition could they find in her holds. There were some red faces, I can tell you. Meanwhile, I need hardly say, the wee *Clyde Valley* was sailing, all innocent-like, into Larne harbour. Loyal hands soon unloaded the thirty thousand guns and the four million rounds of ammunition, and they were on their way to Protestant Volunteers all over the north."

Willie James looked lovingly at the gun in the corner. Then he poured boiling water into the teapot.

"I've never heard the like," said Uncle Robert.

"Every word of it is true as God's my witness," said Willie James. "You see, when it comes to organisation, nobody can beat us. And do you know why? It's because we're in the right of it."

He went over to the corner of the kitchen and picked up the Hamburg rifle.

"The Germans are the great craftsmen," he mused. "A pity we ever had to fight them."

As my Uncle Robert and I plodded homewards through the twilight, I brooded on the story I had heard. I could imagine armed men lurking behind every Tyrone bush. From every meadow came the sound of UVF men drilling. I heard the distant crackle of gunfire. I heard voices raised in anger. I heard screams of pain as men fell mortally wounded.

I imagined we were in a foreign land—like the Tyrone countryside through which my uncle and I trudged our way towards home, yet somehow new and strange to my experience—

115

where the UVF men had gone to take part in a fight against another enemy whose chief was called the Kaiser. German guns had been turned on Germans. It was all very confusing.

"Willie James is a big talker," said Uncle Robert, breaking in on my reverie. "Some would say he's only an oul' bletherer. Of course, he's never fired that precious gun of his in anger and I hope he never will."

I began to wonder whether there would be war in my time as Uncle George had prophesied. Would there be darkness at noon? Would the green fields turn red with human blood?

Time would tell.

THIRTEEN

In Search
of Bonar Thompson

Students of 20th-century British politics will know the name of
Bonar Law who served in Lloyd George's coalition during the
First World War and formed a Conservative government in
1922. I understand that, though born in New Brunswick, Canada,
Bonar Law had north of Ireland antecedents. All that concerns
me with him, however, is the name Bonar. It came to have
significance for me.

One warm summer day in about 1936, I was rummaging
through the shelves of the little lending library (hired from
Eason's, the wholesale newsagents) that was one of the sidelines
in the newsagent's run by my Aunts Tillie and Annie on the
Stranmillis Road, not far from the Botanic Gardens in Belfast.
(My aunts, demonstrating the fabled Presbyterian thrift my
father had so pointedly lacked, had worked themselves up from
the rough-and-tumble of Broadway in the west of the city to the
more genteel and cosmopolitan university area.)

Most of the books were detective novels, thrillers, romantic
fiction—in short, rubbish turned out by literary huxters. Then
I caught sight of a spine—*Hyde Park Orator*. Intrigued, I opened
the book to find an introduction by Sean O'Casey. I removed it
stealthily and, putting it under my blue-monogrammed school
jacket, crept upstairs with it to my book-lined room. The author
was someone called Bonar Thompson.

Thompson proved to be a man from the Glens of Antrim who had lived through many a picaresque adventure. He had ended up, after a series of stop-gap jobs, as an acidly witty commentator on life with a capital 'L', at Speakers' Corner near Marble Arch. He wore a wide-brimmed black hat to symbolise his authority as 'Prime Minister of Hyde Park'. (Did he get the idea, I wonder, from the comedian George Robey who advertised himself as 'the Prime Minister of Mirth'?) He had started a weekly newspaper called *The Black Hat*, which ran for nine issues.

Bonar obviously had much of the actor in him as well as the salesman's instinct. At one time, he had tried to make his fortune from selling contraceptives. Now he sold wit as a minuscule Bernard Shaw, except that he had abandoned socialism for what may be termed nihilism. Thompson was the forerunner of the *Private Eye*-type of satire. This was spiced with his own cheeky brand of Ulster sauce.

At the end of his blarneying, Thompson took a 'silver collection' outside the gates of the park. This venue was forced on him by police regulations—though, of course, it diminished his earnings as only the truly thankful would follow him at the end of his spiel to reward him with a silver coin. Having read *Hyde Park Orator*, I decided that as soon as good fortune or clever management made a visit to London possible, I should make straight for Hyde Park to marvel at this genius of the soapbox.

Mother and my aunts often talked of Uncle Johnny who had gone to Liverpool, aged fourteen, to serve his time in the grocery business and who now—so they believed—was a thriving merchant in Birmingham. Time had eroded the family bonds for John McCrea and it was some years since they had news of him.

Occasional letters and Christmas cards were despatched across the Irish Sea, but Birmingham sent no answering signal. Was he ill? Supposing he died and they did not hear of his death? Uncle Johnny had always been given a wonderful build-up. He was, in short, everything that father was not: the sober, industrious apprentice who, as a lad of fourteen, had gone forth to make his way in the world.

Now it was thought he had reaped his reward in cash and possessions, was a man respected by all and not least by his bank manager. Had not young Johnny been the bravest and most honest boy who had ever drawn breath? Had he not, until ill-luck came in the form of his wife's invalidism, been a generous and devoted brother?

In the late autumn of 1936, I saw an advertisement in the *Belfast Telegraph* announcing a cheap excursion to Liverpool for football supporters. Here was my chance to get to Birmingham. I visited Thomas Cook's in Royal Avenue for the first time and asked them to make arrangements. To Birmingham would I go on pilgrimage to seek out the much-talked-about and long-lost John McCrea, grocer and Freemason, the Derry orphan who had prospered.

I called in at the Reference Library in Royal Avenue and did my homework. A scrutiny of *Kelly's Directory* provided me with the address in Birmingham—219 Poplar Avenue, Edgbaston. I already knew his shop was in near-by Waterloo Road. I embarked full of zest for this would be my first visit to England, an unknown country. So far I had only been 'across the water', as we said, to Scotland.

I got to Liverpool and then Crewe and then Birmingham and, at last, I stood in Uncle Johnny's shop in Waterloo Road. I was just a tiny bit disappointed that he was not more welcoming to his nephew whom he had last seen as a small child. But there he was, caught in the commercial act of bending over his bacon-slicing machine, white-aproned, chunky, full-cheeked and grey-haired. He turned out to be a sensible, right-minded small businessman of strong Conservative and anti-trade union views. Before I left to catch my train at New Street, he handed me a crinkled pound note. But, more important, he asked me to come and stay at his house the following summer.

I returned to Belfast a wise and more travelled boy than when I left. I was pleased to be able to tell my pals at school of my visit to the English midlands, for at that time few had ventured outside the north of Ireland. The era of the package tour lay in the distant future. I spoke of the immensity of Crewe station with its multiplicity of platforms and silver curving tracks and signal boxes. What mattered most, however, was the invitation to return. Then, I knew, I would go to London for the day and on a Sunday so that I could see and hear Bonar Thompson, Hyde Park Orator extraordinary.

The months passed quickly from grey, short-dayed winter into spring with its promise—sometimes unkept—of warmth and long walks along the tow-path to Shaw's Bridge with friends with whom confidences could be exchanged. Or I would go for a ride on my new Raleigh sports bike that had cost all of £4.19s.11d. I would push, push, push deep into the country, dreaming ... dreaming ... and usually with a Penguin book in my pocket. I was waiting as patiently as I could for the delights of suburban Edgbaston and visits to Warwickshire and Worcestershire that Uncle Johnny had promised. Though not particularly attractive, Birmingham was immense and I looked forward to exploring a city in which nobody would know me.

At school, boys began to talk of what lay in store for them. Some were worried since secure jobs, like money itself, 'did not grow on trees'. I had another couple of years to go and did not worry over-much about what would happen to me. I would survive somehow.

"I'm going to be articled in my father's firm," Dixon would say.

His father was an accountant. How boring, I thought.

"Business for me, there's good money in it, and no more bloody exams," Wilson would put in.

"I've always wanted to be a teacher," Ferguson, a pale, studious boy, a swot, as we called him, would tell his friends.

I got used to hearing the question from adults, "What are you going to do with yourself?"

I could hardly answer that I wanted to write. That would have been quite unacceptable, so I found a formula that went down well. I tried to keep a straight face as I said gravely, 'The Civil Service'.

It sounded respectable and gave the impression that I had given the matter some concentrated thought. There was the local civil service at Stormont and the Imperial in London, so if further pressed I would say with an air of grandeur, "The Imperial, of course". I imagined that Imperial civil servants lived a life of luxury, all Turkish carpets and soft lights.

For weeks before the end of term, I could smell the ripe odour of Birmingham's fruit market, not dissimilar to that in Belfast, but much vaster. This time I would not be travelling with a mob of Guinness-swilling football fans, but as a tourist. No adventurer set forth for the New World with more eagerness than I did for the English midlands, that I hoped would not be, in Hilaire Belloc's words, "sodden and unkind".

Uncle Johnny, a widower, was looked after by a housekeeper who also helped in the shop. I was given a bedroom in his Edgbaston villa that seemed to come right out of the catalogue pages of the Times Furnishing Company's showrooms in the centre of the city. Being a busy man, Uncle Johnny had not a great deal of time to devote to his Irish nephew, but he did do his best to show me the local sights and, on one Sunday, drove me into the lush Worcestershire countryside. I made some excursions on my own, to the zoo in Dudley which I reached after passing through dirty and foul run-down areas, and to Stratford-upon-Avon, a smiling, middle-class English town where I saw a production of *The Tempest* and ate Walls' ice-cream.

On another Sunday, I left Snow Hill station on a day trip to London where I hoped one day to settle, be a writer and live with a foreign woman to whom I was not married. Alas for dreams! I did live there for many years with the wife I married in Fisherwick Presbyterian Church in Belfast. But I digress. Arrival at Paddington brought me into the pre-war metropolis and an atmosphere that now is as historic as the fog-enveloped city of Charles Dickens. I walked through the broad streets, then into Bayswater Road and finally through chance and design got to Speakers' Corner in Hyde Park. Later I would have to take a quick look at Buckingham Palace or else be prepared to lie to my mother and aunts back home, for Buck House was the only building in London of any interest to them.

At Speakers' Corner they were all there in force—the Salvation Army, the Coloured Workers' League, the Independent Labour Party, the Peace Pledge Union, Catholic Truth Society, the James Connolly Association and the indefatigable Dr. Donald Soper. Tongues wagged, hecklers interrupted. *Words, words, words.* Then I caught sight of the object I was looking for—a black hat. This was perched on the head of a middle-aged man who had gathered a small band around him. There, indeed, was Bonar Thompson, the oratorical champ from the Glens of Antrim. I advanced to join his *al fresco* Bible Class which he addressed in an accent that still had traces of the Glens.

Thompson's style differed markedly from that of his fellow-speakers. He was quiet, self-contained. In fact, he was not so much an orator as simply a good and persuasive speaker whose silver tongue was never at a loss for a pithy or caustic comment. Here was a man who espoused no cause. Having abandoned socialism, he preached no gospel, religious or secular. He cast a cold eye on politicians and propagandists of all stripes, and served up a piping hot commentary spiced with wit and humour, a man-in-the-street's GBS.

He undertook to talk about everything under the sun, but obviously enjoyed giving his anarchic version of the week's news. The Antrim man claimed to take his listeners behind the scenes, whether in the British Cabinet room or Buckingham Palace. He was at home in both the Kremlin and the Vatican.

"Anthony Eden," he confided, "was the best advertisement the Fifty Shilling Tailors ever had." Then he turned his attention to the police who were apparently not among his closest friends. He told us how to recognise policemen in plain clothes—"By their boots ye shall know them." He pointed out that London buses carried the notice: "Spitting Prohibited: Penalty 40s" whereas in the British Museum a notice said: "Spitting Prohibited: Penalty 20s." The moral, he maintained, was that if one must spit, then it should be done in the British Museum.

Like many Irishmen of his generation, Bonar Thompson—despite coming from what he calls in his autobiography "the poorest of the Ulster peasantry"—was extremely well-read. He could quote from Shakespeare, Dickens and O'Casey at the drop of his own black hat. I was not alone in being one of his admirers. Michael Foot, a former leader of the Labour Party, has written in his *Debts of Honour* of Thompson. "I learnt from him," Foot tells us, "much useful or, better still, useless knowledge which, as they say, stood me in good stead ever after." Thompson died in 1963, after a hard and unrewarding life, aged seventy-five. Characteristically, he chose a suitable epitaph for himself, bearing in mind the regulations of the Metropolitan Police. It reads 'The collection was not enough'.

One by one the speakers on that pre-war Sunday afternoon got down off their platforms and stood on the flat earth before departing for another week. The captains and the kings of harangue—if not the art of Demosthenes—faded away in the anonymity of what was then the capital of the British Empire. I walked aimlessly in Hyde Park and gaped at the couples lying on the grass and clasped in that attitude of timelessness that enfolds lovers. They could lie more carefree than similar couples in puritanical Belfast, where even children's playgrounds were locked fast against Sunday pleasure.

Then a voice sounded beside me.

"'ullo dear, lookin' for someone?"

The voice was husky and cockney. Behind it lay a suggestion of invitation and menace. I was overpowered by the odour of cheap perfume. I was speechless, never having been approached in that way before.

"First time in London, dearie?"

"Yes," I stammered. "How did you guess?"

The woman was heavily made up—blonde, coarsely over-lipsticked and with rouge on her cheeks. She looked middle-aged, but probably was under forty.

"Wot's your name, dear?"

"Henry," I said, giving father's name.

"'enery ... I've known some 'eneries in my time, I 'ave. Cheeky buggers, most of 'em. Like to come 'ome with me, 'enery?"

"I ... I don't know. I've a train to catch at Paddington."

She tittered.

"I can see as 'ow yer a busy man, love," said the blonde.

Suddenly, she came over and put her arms around me. She kissed me as I had not been kissed before.

"That won't cost you nuffin this time, love ... Next time you 'ave ter pay for it," she muttered. In a moment she was gone.

When I got back to Belfast I wrote in my diary: "The visit to Birmingham was a great success—London even more so. Bonar Thompson was all I expected. As for London itself, it is everything I have imagined—and more."

The dream of things to come now seemed to be taking shape. I knew that I would leave Belfast and never go back. The dream of living in London enchanted me. I knew in my heart that, come what may, I would follow my dream.

FOURTEEN

Tomorrow Evening about Eight

I came back from school, where I was in my last year, and put my bike away in the shed in the back yard. It was a bright, mild June day, almost cloudless in a way we seldom experienced in the north, where the low clouds—so low that one could nearly stand on a ladder and touch them—hardly ever disappeared. The school day had been like most school days, mildly boring, slightly tiresome. I was nearing the end of my school career. I had started, I hoped not too late, to make an effort in Maths and Physics but without any real interest in the subjects. I was rapidly developing a passion, an obsession for something else.

Mother came in briskly from the shop.

"I'm glad you're back, Robbie. There's a telegram for you."

"A what?" I said. "Who would send *me* a telegram?"

"Well," said mother, "I hope it's nothing to do with politics. Politics only gets people into trouble. You just mind your lessons and leave politics to them that has nothing better to do."

"Cut out the speeches, mother," I said. "You're not on a soap box down at the Custom House steps. I'm not either—not *yet*! Now where's the telegram?"

She fished it out from behind Granny McCrea's photo on the mantelpiece. I noticed my surname was misspelt—as usual. I ripped it open and read: COME TOMORROW EVENING ABOUT EIGHT STOP FORREST REID.

I jumped in the air—or at least I think I did. Then I hugged mother fiercely.

"You're very affectionate today," she said, smiling.

"I've only one problem," I said. "I can't decide whether to be the next socialist Prime Minister or the Poet Laureate."

"What a lot of fool talk," she said, though still looking pleased. "I don't know where you get all these strange ideas. It isn't from my side of the family. We're all sane."

The implication was that some of father's relatives were not.

I showed her the telegram. "I've never heard of this Mr. Reid—I hope he's respectable and goes to church on a Sunday?"

"Respectable," I said with contempt. "The man is famous—everywhere except in his native city, that is. He certainly isn't a *petit bourgeois.*"

"You may know a wee bit of French," said mother, "but that doesn't mean you have an iota of sense. Anyway, I hope this Mr. Reid isn't a Sinn Feiner or a communist."

"He's apolitical," I said. "He's a man who writes books."

"Well," admitted mother, "that's not as bad as I thought, but I've heard it said that these writer fellows are hardly ever sober. Now if he offers you alcohol, refuse it."

I was in a daze. A telegram no less! An invitation from a famous writer! Though I never had much of a voice for singing I burst into song:

You've heard of General Wellington, who won at Waterloo,
But there's a good old Irishman I'll mention unto you,
He comes from dear old Dublin, he's a man we all applaud,
For he always finds a corkscrew more handy than the sword.
He's good old General Guinness, he's a soldier strong and 'stout',
Found on every 'bottle-front' and he can't be done without.
His noble name has world-wide fame, for every heart he cheers,
Good old General Guinness of the Dublin 'booseliers'.

"I wonder what your headmaster, Mr. Henderson, would say if he saw you now," said mother, laughing.

"My dear old headmaster, Mr. Henderson," I replied, "wouldn't touch Guinness with a Lagan barge pole. Nothing for him—good Scotsman that he is—but the finest Scotch malt."

When I had been at the elementary school, we were asked to write an occasional composition. To my surprise, this was the easiest bit of work we were ever given—so much easier than the tiresome columns of long addition sums, as if anyone other than grocers really cared what they added up to, anyway. I delighted in words and tried to learn new ones, long ones, strange ones, rich and rare ones. I marvelled at the effect words had on others. Short, vulgar or obscene ones had an enormous effect as when someone called a boy a 'bastard' or 'wee skitter' or chalked the word 'fuck' on the wall of a urinal. Long, learned ones, like 'exasperation', drew exclamations of surprise, even pleasure, from the dour taskmasters who were our teachers.

A master once handed me back a composition and said, "You write like Dickens". From that moment I determined to be a writer in addition to whatever else I should become. For all I knew, the master was merely indulging in sarcasm. The speaker was either a Mr. Harbinson or a Mr. McCullough (the latter being the dark, sardonic vice-principal of the school). The face and name have vanished, the words remain. *Words, words, words—* how they could charm away the devils of fear and depression, especially when they were printed words.

Belfast, unlike Dublin, could hardly be called a city of wits and poets, though indeed we had a few dedicated spirits. The hand of Protestantism had grasped our community firmly and made it worthy if not virtuous, hard-working and thrifty. The 'Black Man' statue outside the grammar school, the Academical Institution, known popularly as 'Inst.', symbolised the Victorian attitudes that, in the 1930s, still prevailed. (The statue, still there, is of an eminent divine, Dr. Henry Cooke, and has been darkened by the elements—hence the name given it.)

As I say, despite the inhospitable atmosphere, a few writers had managed to survive. There was Robert Lynd, the gentle essayist and convert to home rule, whose father had been minister at May Street Presbyterian Church. Lynd had found success in London. Rumour had it that he was a hard drinker who once said to a fellow-boozer in a Fleet Street tavern, "Do you realise that we are the kind of men our mothers warned us against?" My mother—simple soul though she was—had a point and I knew it.

Forrest Reid, then, was *the* literary artist living amongst us: a novelist and autobiographer who wrote for a minority, something perhaps of a cult figure. Sometimes, after the final ring of the school bell, I used to ride off on my bike to Smithfield—now long gone—to browse among the second-hand books in Hugh Greer's and rummage in the fourpenny and sixpenny boxes. It was there by some lucky chance or, more realistically, by a process of seeking and therefore finding, that I came across Forrest Reid's *Apostate* in which he looks back on his childhood and youth. I read these words:

Sunday became to me a veritable nightmare, casting its baleful shadow even over the last hours of Saturday. I hated Sunday, I hated church, I hated Sunday School, I hated Bible stories, I hated everybody mentioned in both the Old and New Testaments, except perhaps the impenitent thief, Eve's snake, and a few similar characters. And I never disguised these feelings. From dawn till sunset the day of rest was for me a day of storm and battle, renewed each week, and carried on for years with a pertinacity that now seems hardly credible, till at length the opposition was exhausted and I was allowed to go my own way.

This, indeed, was a soul speaking unto a kindred soul. I, too, had waged such a battle, and I too, in the end, had been allowed to go my own way. The street corner evangelists would have consigned me to the flames of hell as readily as they would any Papist. I, who had been granted the opportunity to know better! At last I knew that in rebelliousness there had been at least one forerunner, a member of the writing tribe.

How thrilling it was to discover a writer whose pages had imprinted on them familiar names such as Mount Charles, the University Road and the Botanic Gardens, for it was precisely this area of Belfast, the immediate vicinity of my grammar school, for which I had the deepest affection. I turned the pages of *Apostate*, lost in a reverie of delight as paragraph after paragraph spoke to me.

This one, for instance:

There was the beauty of an autumn afternoon in the Ormeau Park at dusk, when, with the dead leaves thick on the deserted paths, I had sat listening to a German band playing somewhere out of sight of the railings. Through the twilight, with its yellow twinkling of street lamps, the music had floated. The tune was the old *Lorelei*, but into the plaintive twang of those instruments all the melancholy of the earth had passed. It was as if the very soul of the empty park had found a voice, and were sobbing out its complaint to the November sky.

The assistant in Greer's came up and gave me a hard look.

"You've been readin' that wee book a quare long time," he said. "It's gettin' on for closin' time. Are you thinkin' of buyin' it?"

"Yes," I said.

In this way, a new name came into my consciousness. Forrest Reid, one of my teachers told me, still lived in Belfast, out at Knock, he believed. Up to that time, I thought all writers lived in London or perhaps down south in Dublin. The teacher also told me that Reid had once gone out to a local shop in his pyjamas—such was the daftness of writers. With all speed, I ransacked the Public Library in Royal Avenue for Reid's other books, the novels *Uncle Stephen, Brian Westby* and *Following Darkness* (the last renamed *Peter Waring* a few years later) and read them avidly.

But the novels, unlike *Apostate*, disappointed me. They seemed, for all their lyrical charm and their fastidious sentence construction, to be too limited. Nobody I had read so far had written so sensitively of childhood and, more particularly, boyhood, but, outside the magic years of adolescence, Forrest Reid seemed to be at a loss. His adults did not ring true. At the time I sensed this but did not know why, for homosexuality was something I knew nothing about, not even the word itself. And yet, I had to admit that for me Reid was one of the great men— the only great man, perhaps—living in our matter-of-fact and all too philistine city.

I looked Reid up in *Who's Who* in the Central Library. He had been educated at Inst. and Cambridge. The university in Belfast had conferred an honorary doctorate on him. He was a keen croquet player. Like our city, I was matter-of-fact on one point. I wanted his address and there it was in *Who's Who*—13 Ormiston Crescent. Having lately acquired a Remington portable type-writer, second-hand at five pounds, I typed out, as best I could, several of my poems and a short story, and wrote a letter that started:

Dear Mr. Reid,
Having read much of your work with admiration, I, a school-boy with the ambition to become a writer, am taking the liberty of sending you some examples of my poetry and fiction.

Forrest Reid replied, in a remarkably neat hand, to the effect that he had read my manuscripts with interest and that they showed 'promise'. Would I like to call on him some evening so that he could discuss them with me? I replied that any evening would suit me fine. Hence the telegram.

On that memorable Tuesday evening, within a minute or two of eight, I reached Ormiston Crescent. I got off my Raleigh sports bike and walked gingerly past No. 13. He had said 'about eight' so I walked to the end of the street and then back again to the pebble-dashed little house that was No. 13. In my naïvety, I had supposed that a famous novelist would live in a large house with a long drive up to the front door. There one would ring the bell and be admitted by a butler straight out of P.G. Wodehouse. "What name shall I give, sir?" he would enquire in BBC announcer tones. Then I would be ushered into the study where the novelist himself, in evening dress, would be clutching an extremely dry martini. He would offer me one and I would refuse politely, explaining that I had a sore throat. But here was a house smaller than the one inhabited by my non-famous Uncle Johnny in Edgbaston—Uncle Johnny who had left school at fourteen and now sliced bacon and weighed out tea for a living. Life was full of surprises.

I rang the bell. Instead of a butler in tails, out came Forrest Reid himself. A man in casual tweeds, he held a pipe awkwardly and peered at me through thick-lensed glasses as if he were a sensitive, easily-frightened animal.

"Come in," he said, politely.

In I went to make the acquaintance of the most famous man in Belfast.

He thanked me for letting him see my work and he talked about it. Yes, definitely promising but rather derivative. Didn't I think so myself? What writers had I been reading? Did I know the poetry of his friend de la Mare? Had I read Yeats? I muttered something about liking 'Innisfree' and he smiled. Had I said something wrong? I mentioned Swinburne and then proceeded to quote Tennyson. He corrected me gently and I could have bitten my tongue. Literature, he told me, needed work ... concentration ... dedication.

I said I was a socialist. He replied that politics did not interest him. Politicians were loud people, vulgar, often insincere. The European situation was menacing. He said he loathed the Germans and their abominable Fuhrer, who couldn't even speak German properly, and that—apart from Goethe—German writers of note had all been Jews. The room in which this conversation took place contained more books than I had ever seen in a private house. How was it possible for a man to gather, let alone read, so many? He made tea which we drank out of

131

delicate china. No wine, whiskey or martinis were offered, so I was spared the embarrassment of refusal. "Come again," he said kindly, "and do send me some more of your poems and stories."

So it was that my first writer turned out to be avuncular and intelligent, but unlike any of my real uncles. As I rode home, I felt that somehow they were, in their rough, homespun way, more real as people, more manly. Forrest Reid was what? A private man, yes, a private man who allowed only a few to cross the threshold into his interior world. Belfast knew him not and he had no wish to know Belfast. But what had I expected from him? Some kind of lightning flash that would illuminate the whole of life? The boy who rode away from Ormiston Crescent was a somewhat different one from the boy who arrived with glowing face and high hopes on a close June evening.

True, I went back two or three times to the little house and its book-lined study always fascinated me. Perhaps I warmed to Reid's vast assembly of books more than I warmed to Reid himself. He seemed to be hiding away in a world beyond my reach. In later years, we exchanged a few letters and he kindly contributed to a couple of anthologies I edited. He sent me a warm note of congratulation on my marriage, an institution, I imagine, for which he had scant regard. But soon after these visits I found new literary gods. One of these was the Viking god reincarnated as Wystan Hugh Auden.

Yet all these years after meeting Forrest Reid, I find pleasure in recalling that I knew, however slightly, the author of *Apostate*. Nor do I forget that the young Reid once saw Oscar Wilde—an unlikely figure among the linen merchants and the shipyard workers of Belfast—climb up and sit beside the coachman on the box seat of a carriage. Culpable escapism no doubt, but I cannot help longing in this noisy, polluted age for the placid days of Forrest Reid's boyhood when the Linen Hall still existed and the inner suburbs were almost rural and "the few horse trams, their destination indicated by the colour of their curtains, did little to disturb the quiet of the streets".

FIFTEEN

The Goddess that Failed

I spent my childhood and adolescence in Belfast. Self-righteous young Presbyterian and would-be sensualist, I walked those everlastingly damp streets. There I was first visited by the creative impulse, wayward, undeniable, long before I had written a line of poetry. Listen. Suppose it is a spring evening, the lamps not yet lit, mysterious, full of tender whispers, the shadows massing, and the trees along Botanic Avenue quivering gently in the silk air. I have been out walking alone, thinking the long and unfulfillable thoughts of youth, gaping at girls but speaking to nobody, stirred by a young melancholy, half-wistful, half-divine.

A red tram, with an open upper deck, clangs along and I enjoy its boisterous show of noise, its shouting that it is alive though factually it is inanimate. A policeman in his dark-green uniform clumps by, revolver on hip, a reminder that we live in a bitterly divided society. A group of respectable citizens pass, talking in a subdued way, indistinct, afraid to speak up as if they were afraid to be overheard and reported to some secret police force.

I bounce along brimming over with life, floating 'down the rivers of the windfall light'. I am in love with being in love. Years later, I would read and recognise myself in the words of André Gide who says that, in the spring, "the ardent adolescent, tormented by an unknown restlessness, leaves his scorching bed to go in quest of the mystery".

This evening our work-a-day town wears a wanton and brash beauty. Warehouse and factory chimney and ship funnel and gasometer are seen as if for the first time and they are out of time. Now, outside the prison of school, I tell myself I, yes I, am young and alive. The gift of life is wonderful and one cannot be too grateful for it. I repeat my name inwardly and it seems strange, foreign, exotic. But what of my future? Would anyone be interested in my thoughts, my images, my word rhythms? I could but try.

An artistic vocation is one thing, a career quite another. I did not know what do with myself so far as a career was concerned, for the only thing I cared for was thinking my own rebellious and estatic and lonely thoughts, and strolling over bridge and quayside and through the markets, watching life flow round and over me. Well, well, they told me there was no career in writing down such daftness ... who would read such stuff ... no security for one's old age, no pension. No, there was positively no career in letters—unless one became a postman, ha-ha! Not like working in a nice bank, or teaching in a nice school (such good holidays, you know) or doing one of the other thousand and one jobs guaranteed to make even the most gay and daring spirit mediocre. Obviously I was not going to become a good citizen, a respectable elder of the Presbyterian church and so on; I would be a dead loss to myself and everyone else and a sore disappointment to my schoolmasters, who assured me I could be as conformist as the next boy *if only I tried.*

I had sat for a Bank examination and been let down by my lack of knowledge of the mathematical sciences; and if I but knew, perhaps, some of the subversive but to me very natural ideas that crept into my examination essay had rightly led an examiner to realise that my talent, unlike that of the young T.S. Eliot, would not flower best at the receiving side of a polished mahogany or oak counter. I cannot recall the precise reason why I failed to make a debut in the assured world of Marine, Accident or Life Insurance: once again my naïvety told its own tale to an astute businessman. Oh well, I thought, I would just have to go to the

134

local university, until penny-a-line journalism would receive me, for one or two local editors had been vaguely encouraging, saying they might have taken me on but for anticipated war-time shortage of newsprint. Snags, frustrations, too young here, too old there, too clever, not clever enough ... yet in the end, I felt, with a little bit of luck, something would turn up, even if it was not exactly what I had longed for.

The 1930s ended on September 3rd, 1939, not on December 31st of that year. We were at war with Germany, a fact Chamberlain announced unheroically, undramatically, tired resignation in his voice. "A low, dishonest decade", in W.H. Auden's words, was over. On that Sunday when war started, it thundered and lightning'd in the hills ringing Belfast. The voice of God or the vast bass rumble of Aryan man asserting world supremacy? *Ein Volk, Ein Reich, Ein Fuhrer!* How well we knew that voice which had often invaded our homes through the air waves.

Were the street evangelists, with their hoarse cries, right in suggesting that anti-Christ was upon us? "Prepare to meet Thy God" might be more than a Biblical quotation scrawled on brick walls. Had my Uncle George—farmer, philosopher, prophet of doom, isolationist, bachelor misogynist, tinkerer with agricultural machinery and red-nosed introvert who launched a thousand silences—been right after all in his prophecy that civilisation was on the way out?

On that still-remembered Sunday of September 3rd, 1939, I went to church to please my aunts who were worshippers at Fisherwick, a massive Presbyterian church of unusual dignity. I pondered the words "Thou shalt not kill", for now I knew that in the Ulster Protestant community the killing of Germans would be considered praiseworthy. Yet I could not help wondering whether Christ had not preached pacifism and—to the dismay of some of his followers—the quiet acceptance of foreign domination. I felt that such doubts I should keep to myself. Our community was not one that welcomed criticism of its values. It continued to live under siege and was inclined to equate criticism, however well-meant, with betrayal.

Here I was, rapidly growing out of my teens and in love with life, and in love with love, and awakening to both sensuous and sensual delight. This surely was no time to hug the death-wish that reflected the collective unconscious. I kept telling myself that in the end life could, *must* conquer. Rumours abounded. It was said that a bomb existed which, dropped on the City Hall, would destroy the whole city, a prefiguring of the atomic destruction visited upon Japan several years later.

I had read and been told about the war of 1914-18 and tended to assume that history was about to repeat itself. I expected mass hysteria would slowly develop. Would I too succumb in time and join the war-dance in the black-out? To me the only answer was that if I kept on writing I might be able to remain detached and sane. Writing seemed to be a necessary therapy which, if frustrated, would lead to mental numbness and inner death. As T.S. Eliot put it, "I would not know what I thought until I saw what I wrote".

That September was a painful and critical month for me. This was partly due to depression caused by the outbreak of a war I long knew to be inevitable and partly due to my own trauma at the time. Irene, goddess of peace, had said 'No', and I felt as if my emotional structure was crumbling. 'No' shouted the angry gods, as the leaves fell heedlessly from a brooding sky. I wandered restless, apparently defeated before the struggle had started, hurt and rebellious but drained of energy, obsessed with futile sexual fantasies and doomed to non-conformist frustration. Under the shadow of Cavehill and Divis, along the towpath to Shaw's Bridge where hardy swimmers still plopped Adam-naked in the cool Lagan, around the big tinsel-laden stores in the city centre, in the dusty second-hand bookshops of Smithfield, back and forth from the Stranmillis Road to Belgravia Avenue off the Lisburn Road (where my old school friend, Leslie Baxter, lived) feverishly intent on long-forgotten enterprises of work and play I hastened, while the world cocked its ear and waited for the crunch of bombs and the moans of the injured. Or I would go up the Antrim Road to Brookhill Avenue and glance at the dignified, if non-descript, brick house inhabited by my beloved blonde Irene. I consulted a doctor who diagnosed my complaint as 'nervous dyspepsia'. As for my chronic catarrh, he advised me to emigrate to Canada as soon as I had the opportunity. O God! O Montreal!

Irene may merely seem a figure of speech to conjure up the Greek goddess who failed to preserve peace in 1939. In fact she was a real—only too intensely real—person and I have not changed the name. She was a blonde, tall, slight-breasted girl, greatly interested in literature but neither doomed nor buoyed up by literary aspiration. She had read some of my poems and articles with approval and, to my delight, expressed the opinion that some of them were up to publication standard. She introduced me to the BBC weekly, *The Listener*, which printed poems that did not necessarily use rhyme schemes. Irene and I discussed poetry from Wordsworth to Dylan Thomas and Louis MacNeice, and as my admiration for her blossomed so did my love. She was my pale shepherdess. But now she had cast me out of her life in favour of a man who, I understood, was an engineering student.

Most men thrive when they are 'believed in' by women they respect; and it is a heavy blow to find that belief arbitrarily withdrawn so that the world of reality is no longer cushioned by affection. Then one sadly realises that one's only friend in this harsh world is oneself. All the more poignant, at the outset of life, to find a flower and later see it wither in one's hand. Yet the life-will somehow asserts itself and the caravan of the ego moves ruthlessly on. Nevertheless, the shock to the personality can take years to wear off. I cannot even now be sufficiently exhibitionistic to explain the hows and whys of Irene's repudiation. That it did happen must be sufficient for the purpose of this narrative. And so, I enrolled reluctantly in the Faculty of Arts of Queen's

University, Belfast, for war had shut all the other doors into the great world I longed to enter. I wrote, wrote, wrote. Words formed into oblongs and squares and diamonds that were poems. Could words in some magical way call back mankind to love and reason? It seemed doubtful but one could at least try to pass on to others the intensities and depths in being alive. Despite the near-suicidal fits of despair that came unbidden life was still worth going on with.

Irene's defection, apart from depression and 'nervous dyspepsia', prompted me to write a poem I simply called 'Love' and which appeared in the Queen's University magazine I was later to edit during a brief and less than brilliant undergraduateship. I wrote:

Love is a wet autumn night
and a youth who walks alone,
whose damp hair is plastered unheeding
like rain-swept leaves on the sullen ground.
It is tears in the eyes
and a woman's automatic politeness,
sorrow for everything and not knowing
why it matters so much,
and getting wet, and not caring,
and walking and walking—alone
—walking aimlessly unloved.

It was in the autumn of 1939, or the beginning of the 'phoney war' winter, that I met Roy McFadden at a discussion group meeting of the local branch of the Peace Pledge Union. He and I had much in common—as indeed we still have. The passing of time has deepened rather than diminished our friendship. Roy had an appealing shy intensity and smouldering anger against all merchants of death and their apologists. His mother, whom

I had come across shortly before I met him, told me of a son who intended to qualify as a solicitor, wrote poetry and opposed the war. Odd, I thought. We exchanged specimens of our work and recognised in each other a wish to write poetry because it was essential to our well-being and not because it was a pleasant hobby to while away the dull, wintry Ulster evenings.

Poetry mattered and life mattered; and we felt anxious to communicate to others, however few they might be, this urgent sense of the inner reality behind the outer reality. Roy's inner reality still rests in that he is a poet; and his outer reality consists in his day-to-day work as a solicitor: an inner and outer world. He manages to fit together the two sides of his personality, and so create for himself a satisfying and vital life-style. In the days when I first got to know him, he was looking for that inner-outer synthesis. His poetry had, I remember, a Keatsian loveliness; it stirred me and yet it only half-appealed. I say 'half-appealed' because I was then beginning to be overwhelmed, almost obsessed, by the idea of contemporaneity. What of the new heroes in my poetic firmament, Eliot, Auden, Spender, MacNeice? Pylons, not daisies! Contemporary ugliness seemed to have its poetic uses, for did not Day Lewis write of 'sour canals'?

I introduced Roy to another new friend of mine, Leslie Gillespie, a Queen's University Honours English student, also a keen writer but one more interested in prose than verse. A stocky, Germanically fair, slightly tough-looking young man, Leslie had enjoyed the battles on the football field in a more robust way than I ever had. He had a great admiration for Ernest Hemingway, whom I only mildly saluted, and whom, I suspect, Roy probably loathed.

I had met Leslie at Queen's. As his surname began with the same initial as mine, we had been placed in the same history class. It was at Queen's that I truly realised that history was about the dead—at Methody figures like Napoleon, Wellington, even the more distant figure of Cromwell, seemed as real to me as Churchill and Stalin. Leslie, in fact, was the first person I had met who expressed the wish to be a writer above all else. He wrote

139

mainly short stories while I wrote poems. Each of us thought the work of the other was good, remarkable, indeed at times we may have even used the word 'inspired'. His belief in the value of my early writing was of great assistance in my gaining self-confidence. If I was a fool—and there seemed to be increasing evidence for that view—then I had found another of the same kind. If I was not a fool—and the occasional letter of acceptance encouraged me to think I might not be—then he and I would go to London and conquer it together. Thus we laid the basis of a firm literary and personal friendship.

He was an extrovert, I, an introvert. It was fortunate I met him for I was in a phase of suicidal despair when Leslie suggested we should spend a few days cycling round the countryside during the Easter vacation, and I was glad to fall in with the suggestion. The war seemed very far away—and indeed it was—and the blonde Irene who 'never wanted to see me again' (and had thereby induced the despair) appeared less of a goddess as Gillespie and I cycled round the Antrim glens and ate our tins of baked beans, fried eggs and bacon at Youth Hostels, and talked ourselves hoarse and to sleep in the early hours—our main topics being (in big capital letters) Life, Death and Being Writers.

In time Roy, Leslie and I formed a trio (later joined by John Gallen) of eager young men turning out poems, critical articles and short stories in a rather sceptical and, at times, even hostile environment. Hostility spurred me on, although I found indifference devastating. During the next couple of years the Queen's University literary magazine, *The Northman*, was at our disposal, edited as it was by John Gallen and myself.

I do not know whether the thesis-writers will every try to gain PhDs based on the literary events and atmosphere of Belfast in the early 1940s. These had an exhilarating tang and led to perhaps more good work than might have been expected in the circumstances. True, the 'three Gs' and Roy incurred dislike in some quarters (especially among their immediate and somewhat Marxist-orientated elders) and a reputation for a certain

140

arrogance. Who were they to set themselves up? They were 'angry young men' long before that catchphrase had been invented. What was worse, they had assumed a strangely non-committal political attitude in the middle of a war which was, so we were told, being fought to ensure the survival of civilised human values. It was all very reprehensible.

I am far from wishing to apologise for the attitude of my early adulthood. I enjoyed the struggle with older and wiser heads that shook sadly and knowingly. Some offence was taken, too, by the undergraduate body at the university which disliked the supposedly cavalier way in which John and I, aided and abetted by Roy and Leslie, decided to make *The Northman* into a journal of reasonable literary quality—'Ulster's only literary magazine' as we called it in showcards displayed by local booksellers. Eventually John and I were ousted from the editorship, but not before we had introduced into the pages of *The Northman* work by various non-Ulster writers then making their name. Among these were Henry Treece and Alex Comfort. Local contributors included Denis Ireland, John Irvine, J.H. Scott and Harold Brooks. We reprinted a furious attack, contained in a letter to me, on a pamphlet I had recently edited, *Poems From Ulster*. This came from an irate St. John Ervine who lived in the far reaches of Devonshire.

Time passed. The phoney war ended. Bombs fell on Belfast—despite the forecasts from wiseacres that we were too far away and too unimportant to be worth the attention of the Luftwaffe—and de Valera sent up the Dublin Fire Brigade to help in rescue work. For myself, I was busy with a number of activities, the least important of which I considered to be my academic ones, with the result that I never finished my degree, although I was later to acquire a Diploma in Social Studies at Trinity College, Dublin. Poems and reviews of mine began to appear in the Dublin *Bell* and the London *Horizon* and elsewhere. Wrey Gardiner, editor of the then influential *Poetry Quarterly*, gave me a lot of encouragement. Through my contact with Wrey, I met the versatile scientist-writer Alex Comfort (then a militant pacifist

141

reading medicine at Trinity College, Cambridge) and the two of us were soon hard at work editing an anthology of contemporary verse for Wrey's brave little war-time venture, the Grey Walls Press. This emerged in 1941 as *Lyra: A Book of New Lyric*, for which we were lucky enough to obtain an introduction by Herbert Read.

I scamped my university work, though I did pass a few exams. My studies were pushed aside as I tackled each new literary venture, whether in actual writing or editorial. Throwing myself into the literary life, I joined the local PEN Club and one way and another got to know various writers and would-be writers. It was at a meeting of the PEN club that I first met the novelist Michael McLaverty who had just published his fine lyric novel, *Call My Brother Back*.

Then in his late thirties, the short but stocky Michael, his hair already receding and brushed flat over his head, could seem almost shy. He had little in the way of jovial banter but in a real exchange of views one was struck by the aptness of his remarks and, most of all, by his evident sincerity. His words were considered and came out in a slight nasal tone. He was a professional in the sense of aiming high artistically but I could not imagine him writing deliberately for money. He supported his family as a teacher. I always supposed that Michael taught science as he had an MSc from Queen's University but former pupils have told me that he largely taught poetry and geometry. Perhaps when headmaster he could teach whatever he pleased. Later, the journalist and fiction writer Jack Holland, a pupil of McLaverty, told me of Michael's great love of geometry and of the encouragement Jack got from him for his writing as a schoolboy. I always think that behind every good writer there is a good teacher. I got to know Michael well despite the gap in our ages—some sixteen years. From time to time I visited him and his wife, Mollie, in their home at Deramore Drive off the Malone Road. They were very hospitable. There I would drink Michael's sherry and listen to him speak of book and authors for I was still at a stage when writing seemed glamorous, magic, and had yet, really, to come across the spite and malice writers often delight in. Michael impressed me by saying he sometimes lit the open fire with old copies of the *Times Literary Supplement*. In those days I revered the *TLS* and like most provincials was over-respectful of its anonymous reviewers. Michael helped me realise that a *TLS* was as fallible as anyone else.

Michael, as I said, at that time had just published *Call My Brother Back*, the most satisfying of his eight novels. Originally entitled *Waste Ground* (a title put paid to by the protests from his London publisher), the novel had the ill luck to appear in 1939, just before the outbreak of the war. A year earlier or a year later would have ensured more publicity for his debut. A few years later, *The White Mare*, a collection of short stories, was published by Rowley's Mourne Press. The short story indeed proved to be Michael's true métier.

I certainly valued Michael's warm friendship and the kind comments he made on my work. A chat with him would always raise one's spirits for, as I said, he was entirely free of the envy and malice only too readily found in the literary world. I was always amused by his suspicious attitude towards Dublin which, in some ways, differed little from that of a typical Orangeman. He showed no interest in Dublin's Augustan beauty or its literary ghosts or its easy-going relaxed character. He tended to think that the city was a trap for the writer who would squander his energies and ideas in tavern talk.

Michael had some recognition from the critics both in these islands and in America, but not as much as he deserved. His books are perhaps too quiet in tone in an age when even serious writers shout obscenities or even tendernesses from the rooftops.

A regular feature in the literary landscape was the university flat of Sam Hanna Bell and Bob Davidson. Saturday evenings there could be fun, when the clans gathered to drink, and discuss books, politics and the theatre, and listen to records, and make a pass at whatever girls were available. As the evening progressed, and the bottles of Guinness were emptied, the discussion would become more and more animated, if possibly less and less factually accurate. Hanna Bell was a fiction writer who later joined the Northern Ireland BBC, as did my friend the playwright and man of letters John Boyd. A schoolteacher, John encouraged me to read widely. It was he, I think, who introduced me to Joyce and Lawrence. Anyone might turn up at the Davidson-Bell ménage, for they had acquired a reputation as good-natured fellows who kept open house to all-comers interested in Left-of-Centre politics and the arts.

As I was a few years junior to them, Bob and Sam may well have regarded me with just a grain of suspicion as a young man who threw his weight about rather more than could be justified. For all that, I cannot remember more than a couple of disagreements. I recall with gratitude their kindness and hospitality to a sometimes moody and cantankerous young man.

Belfast, in its own small way, in the early 1940s established a rather more cosmopolitan atmosphere than in the immediate pre-war period. One of the 'soldier-poets' I met in Belfast was Drummond Allison, who had been a contemporary of Sidney Keyes and John Heath-Stubbs at Oxford. Drummond went to some pains to locate me and get in touch. I believe he discovered my whereabouts from Wesley Lutton, who worked in that cultural hive, Davy McLean's little bookshop in Howard Street. We took a great liking to each other, visiting theatres together and drinking foamy-headed glasses of Guinness in the bars, discussing writing and sex. I liked Drummond for the almost ingenuous way he told me of his envy for me because my poetry was being published more widely than his. Also, it seemed to him that, despite my living in a far-away province of the United Kingdom, I seemed to have been admitted to at least fellow-travelling status by a group of new London poets. All this was news to me, for I had thought I led an isolated, even insulated life, made bearable only by the dropping through my letter-box of copies of *The Bell* and *Horizon* and letters from Wrey Gardiner or Tambimmuttu. I envied Drummond's life at Oxford.

Drummond's mother sent me a copy of his book, *The Yellow Night*, his only book of poems. He had signed his name and written an inscription on a gummed slip before going abroad on active service. She enclosed a note to say that Drummond had been killed in the Italian invasion. It seemed unbelievable that a life of such promise and gaiety—for in our few meetings I had sensed in him a true joy-in-living, despite his dislike of army life—should have ended. In later years I have sometimes talked about him to that scholarly poet, John Heath-Stubbs, in the Queen's Elm in Chelsea or the Catherine Wheel in Kensington. Heath-Stubbs and I could hardly be more dissimilar in background and interests, yet every time I see him my first image is of laughing, brave Drummond Allison and myself riding on top of a bus across the Albert Bridge arguing about the merits of W.H. Auden. Even now, over half-a-century later, I feel strongly that Allison's death left a gap in post-war English poetry.

At this period, perhaps the most well-known literary meeting place for writers and artists was Campbell's coffee house opposite the City Hall. Upstairs there, one could look down, possibly in both senses, on the Common Man jumping on and off tramcars.

Imagine a sunny morning in Campbell's during the Second World War. Belfast has been gashed by the Nazi bombers, khaki-clad figures and their War Department vehicles are everywhere. Civil Defence workers are no longer laughed at for their inactivity. Like London, Belfast is learning to 'take it'. The Yanks are here, some said 'over here, over-paid and over-sexed'. They have started dating the local girls—"Say, whaddya do about sex?" Through the windows at Campbell's, one looks across at the City Hall erected in the full flush of Victorian prosperity by the Protestant bourgeoisie. Its statues and gardens I have known from childhood. The City Hall indeed, like the poor and the war profiteer, is something one puts up with. After the war, perhaps, change may come ... but will the war *ever* end?

But let us return to Campbell's. In comes the soldierly, full-figured and genial-faced Denis Ireland, the essayist and wit, whom some people still call Captain Ireland because of his service in the First World War. He is closely followed by his friend William Conor, who sports a bow-tie that suggests his vocation as a painter. A few minutes pass before the arrival of Richard Rowley—the pseudonym of a businessman called Williams who has started a publishing firm, the Mourne Press, which is devoted to making writers like McLaverty and Hanna Bell better-known. The conversation is crisp, wryly humorous in the throwaway northern fashion. It tends towards practicality rather than abstraction. "How much did they pay for it?" Denis Ireland asks, *apropos* of some literary merchandise broadcast by the Belfast regional station of the BBC.

Then Denis launches into yet another funny story, something about 'hogwash' and Sam Goldwyn, and a Hollywood character who told Denis after some allegedly stupendous event, "You ain't seen nuthin' yet". Denis knows his USA from the time he used to visit the States on behalf of the linen firm run by his family. With some care he avoids politics, though we all know him to be something of a white blackbird, that is, an Ulster Protestant—Presbyterian, in fact—with strong nationalist sympathies, a sort of throwback to the radical Presbyterians of the late 18th century who supported the demands of their Catholic fellow-countrymen for reform. Yet even if he did get on to politics, it would not ruffle anyone here, for Campbell's is an island of tolerance in our bitterly divided community. Dissent is permissible and nobody will drench you with coffee for not saying 'the right thing'.

As the minutes pass, more and more faces appear in the upper room. Friends, acquaintances, rivals look in for a 'wee bit of crack'. Over there stands Joe Tomelty, playwright and manager of the Group Theatre, later to appear in the film version of F.L. Green's novel about the IRA, *Odd Man Out*, and later still to be the victim of a cruel motoring accident that will effectively end his career as writer and actor. But now he is talking with some

146

animation to Sam Hanna Bell whose realistic short stories of Ulster life have been published by the Mourne Press under the title *Summer Loanen*. F.L. Green, the best-selling novelist, an Englishman living the city, limps in, leaning heavily on a stick, chalky-faced behind enormous spectacles. Green, one understands, had a leg severely injured, I never discovered how or where. Everyone remembers Diana Wynyard in the film of Green's *On the Night of the Fire.*

Green starts twitting me about the so-called 'Ulster Renaissance' and then tells me about his latest fiction project. "I'm writing," he says, "what you and your friends should be writing, about the real dramas going on here. You people ignore what's going on on your own doorstep." He gives me a real ticking-off and warns me against the lures of "that God-awful place London with its literary cocktail parties". Laurie Green does not fit in at all with the angry young men, but we find him stimulating. A touch of cantankerousness goes down well in these parts. Plain-speaking passes for integrity.

Over in a corner, a couple of young painters are arguing about paintings recently exhibited by CEMA—letters that stand for Council for the Encouragement of Music and the Arts and the forerunner of the Arts Councils that now exist in Belfast and Dublin. Who is that gentleman whose elegance contrasts with the shabbiness of the arty brigade? Why, none other than Gerry Morrow, a member of that remarkably talented theatrical and literary family. I know his more extravert cousin quite well, 'Larry' Morrow who writes witty profiles in *The Bell* in Dublin where he works as a radio journalist. The scribes talk about war aims and how the city ought to be re-built in a contemporary architectural idiom. The company includes two or three who hope to write the Great Ulster Novel. The conversation turns to the latest offering at the Group Theatre—Ibsen's *Ghosts* with Allan McCelland playing the lead.

Lunch time approaches. The writing men, the arty-crafty boys with long hair and their short-haired girls drift off in search of food or, more likely, drink. Food these days is rationed but with an agricultural hinterland people here mostly do rather better than their counterparts in the big English cities. One can always go down to Dublin for a substantial pre-war meal, anyway. The air is heavy with cigarette and pipe smoke, for nobody yet knows the dangers of smoking. I am, fortunately, a non-smoker because smoking irritates my throat and makes me cough. I sit lost in a dream until a buxom waitress bustles round me collecting cups and crumby plates. "Wake up, you," she snaps. "If you've no work to do, other bodies have." The customer is always wrong. I'm surprised she does not add the clichéd phrase "Don't you know there's a war on?" This is the way sloppy service is excused.

Down the stairs I go and out into the flowing tide of humanity. A couple of books under my arm, I saunter along. My feet, if not my head, bring me to the Central Library in Royal Avenue. My mind crowds with images. I think of all the things I want to do in the next few years—assuming I don't perish in the next blitz (hundreds are already dead and there are empty spaces where bombs fell). One takes one's chance and hopes for the best. As the Chinese say, we live in interesting times.

I think of the poem I have written about Irene—'Love is a wet autumn night'. But I reject the words. The sun is shining and the city is full of pretty girls. The autumn seems a long way off. As I cross the road an American jeep flashes past. It has just missed me by inches. A coal-black G.I. shouts at me in a Deep South accent, "Hi, bud, mind ya step!" I follow a dream in Royal Avenue, Belfast, even in the middle of a great war. Even without Irene.

SIXTEEN

Going South

I can sum up my reasons for going south to Dublin in a word—escape. I was dissatisfied with my personal life in Belfast. I felt oppressed by the general narrowness and philistinism. I wanted new doors to open, new opportunities. I wanted to qualify as a social worker so I would have something to fall back on if I did not succeed as a writer or journalist.

I persuaded my McCrea relatives to finance me at Trinity College, Dublin, where I was prepared to work for a Diploma in Social Studies. This in fact I did, for as I said earlier, I never had any difficulty with exams provided I did a minimum of work for them; and this to date is my sole academic qualification—a small one to be sure but better than nothing I suppose. It seemed to me that social work might be both interesting for me and valuable for others, though indeed since taking the diploma I have only engaged in practical social work in the most marginal way. Even that amount of direct contact with the grimmer facts of life have provided me with a measure of experience that I might not otherwise have had.

When I left Belfast in the autumn of 1943 for Trinity I knew that it was goodbye for ever to the River Lagan. The time had come to venture from home and kin, and from the people who, with all their faults and maddening ways, I loved to the point of heartbreak. Father had rejected me; so had Irene. I decided to leave and never go back except for brief visits—and so it has turned out. I went up to the Antrim Road and had a last look at Irene's house, standing solid and four-square in an area that had been severely bombed. It was with a feeling of loss yet buoyed up, too, by the unshakeable optimism of early manhood that I took my leave of Belfast. Dublin represented to me the kind of life I had once craved on the Newtownards Road as an adolescent—a triumphant *yes*.

Dublin's contrasts appealed to me: the wretchedly poor but spirited people of the slums and the elegantly tweeded Anglo-Irish ladies; the splendid glass of the shops in Grafton Street and the broken fanlights in Mountjoy Square. One noted, too, the Dubliner's ready assumption of his city's—and therefore his own—importance. Wartime Dublin was the most fascinating city in these islands, a beacon of light in the European gloom.

The 'Emergency' in Dublin did not take me by surprise as I had already sampled it during brief weekend visits. I had made friends with the Salkeld family, since Cecil Salkeld had published a poem of mine in a hand-set limited edition of 250 copies. Cecil's mother, Blanaid Salkeld, who had once acted at the Abbey Theatre and also wrote poetry, welcomed me to their house in Morehampton Road, Donnybrook.

Cecil had studied in Germany before the war and brought home to Dublin a German wife, Irma. He was a new experience for me, for I had not met before a man who had grown up in an atmosphere where the arts were taken seriously and professionalism encouraged. I learned that Cecil had been something of a prodigy, having exhibited at the age of sixteen. Now he seemed to spend much of his time in bed, reading, writing, chatting to his many callers, talking of his plans. Sometimes he did get up and set to work, especially in the weeks leading up to an exhibition by the Royal Hibernian Academy, of which he was an associate member.

I would call at his house, walk up the stairs to his room at the top, sit on a chair by the master's bedside and listen to his witty and informed comments on the arts, politics, religion and philosophy interwoven with current gossip. Eventually Cecil would lift himself slowly out of bed, dress quickly and then head, myself in tow, for his local, Reddin's pub. Cecil, more than anyone else in Dublin, became my guide, philosopher and friend. Being still touched with that northern Puritan spirit, I would ration his company, remembering I had a lecture to attend or notes to study.

Years later in 1969, I was to read Kate O'Brien's comment on Cecil shortly after his death: "He was a man of too many gifts—none of them sufficiently strong to control him ... He seemed to me to have a contempt for life—which in a man so gifted was especially sad. The invalidism of his later years was deplorable, but must have been an expression of wounded pride, a refusal to compete ... Yet he must be said to have had a good life."

That Cecil had been showered with gifts was indeed true though, at the time I knew him, I did not sense in him a contempt for life. He did refuse to compete in a race in which he felt that the prizes went to industrious mediocrities and time-servers. Painting was the art for which he had a training and his style was easily recognisable, even to a layman. He dabbled in writing and I remember seeing quite a creditable play of his performed by a group of enthusiastic young actors. It was called *A Gay Goodnight*, a phrase lifted from W.B. Yeats, in which 'gay' is used in the original sense. Cecil knew everyone in the arts in Dublin. Once, in the Bailey, he pointed to a man and told me, "That's Liam O'Flaherty". But O'Flaherty was too drunk for Cecil to approach him. I was very disappointed not to meet the author of *Skerrett* and *The Informer*.

It was around this time that my first collection of poems, *One Recent Evening*, was accepted by the London-based Falcon Press. Headed by a young army officer, Peter Baker, Falcon Press was later to join forces with Wrey Gardiner's Grey Walls Press. The Yorkshire-Irish typographer and poet Séan Jennett left Faber and Faber to join the house.

It was thrilling to sign my first publisher's contract and dream of the day the book would actually be on sale in the shops. As it happened, *One Recent Evening* sold well, for it came out bang in the middle of the war-time boom. My next volume, *The Undying Day* (1948)—handsomely designed by Jennett and containing, I believe, better work—sold wretchedly, probably not more than a hundred copies. Poets obviously do not live by poetry alone.

A close literary and personal friend around this period was Valentin Iremonger, a contemporary who worked in the Department of Education. He and I liked each other's poetry and we liked each other. Val took a keen interest in the theatre and acted in the amateur group which performed Cecil's *A Gay Goodnight.* He introduced me to Mary O'Malley who, years later, started the Lyric Players' Theatre when she went to live in Belfast. I remember Val, his face plastered with make-up, playing Mosca in Ben Jonson's *Volpone.*

Val and I would sometimes go together to see Geoffrey Taylor, who had succeeded Frank O'Connor as poetry editor of *The Bell.* Taylor, formerly Phibbs, had once been one of a *ménage à trois* with Robert Graves and Laura Riding in London but, by the time we knew him, he was a very respectable man-of-letters. Taylor really encouraged young poets and, instead of merely sending a rejection slip, would write letters of instruction and encouragement. Or Val and I would go on visits to the painter-poet Freda Laughton whose husband, John Midgley, son of the northern politician, was serving with the Inniskilling Fusiliers in India.

Together Val and I planned various projects, some of which were translated into reality. One that came off was a selection of our most militant poems—together with some by Bruce Williamson—in a paperback volume we called, rather cheekily, *On the Barricades.* This came out under the imprint of New Frontiers Press and carried Val's address in Tritonville Road in Sandymount. Our blurb ran as follows: "*On the Barricades* has literary—and not political—implications. Its three authors—Robert Greacen, Bruce Williamson and Val Iremonger—give proof of a new vitality in Irish writing, a vitality the older generations will not acknowledge. Here they raise and defend their first barricades against the low standards, facile half-truths and lack of integrity that have for too long rotted the Anglo-Irish spirit." It seems odd to me now that we should have laid such stress on Anglo-Irishness since Val came from Catholic Irish stock and Williamson and I were Belfast Protestants. Though Val was a fluent Irish speaker, he often railed against Irish language activists.

I carried on the imprint more or less on my own for some time and tried to break into publishing. I got together an anthology, *Irish Harvest*, in which were assembled stories, articles and poems by the established Irish writers of the time as well as the newcomers. This venture was backed financially by Maurice Fridberg, a Jewish Dubliner who had done well in bookselling in London and who hoped to set up as a publisher in Dublin after the war. This he did, in fact, using as colophon an hour-glass. His first venture was Frank O'Connor's translation of Brian Merriman's *The Midnight Court*, the 18th-century classic. I still have a copy of the book which bears the inscription, "For Robert—my first publishing effort—with every good wish. Sincerely—Maurice. 1.9.45". I did risk my own money in a venture that actually made a profit. This was a children's book, *Ivan and His Wonderful Coat*, written by Patricia Hutchins and illustrated by the painter Nano Reid. Just after the war, children's books were in short supply and great demand both in Britain and Ireland, and I had no problem in selling every copy. In fact, I did not print nearly enough.

But I was not commercially minded. Had I been so, I might have established myself as a fringe publisher. Publishing in Dublin, unlike today, was then only a minor activity and there was room for an energetic newcomer. Val Iremonger and I had set our sights on higher things than making money. We began to collaborate on putting together an anthology of modern Irish verse. Night after night, we sat in front of a huge turf fire in the sitting room of Val's home in Sandymount and debated the merits of this and that poem, this and that poet. We read incessantly both books and magazines in which living poets had contributions, and together decided, with the minimum of friction, who and what ought to be in. News leaked out that we were in the anthology business and it was confidently asserted in the Dublin pubs that the project would come to nothing. Although we had the ear and eye of T.S. Eliot, through an acquaintance of mine in London, it seemed, after a promising start, that our labours might be in vain. Eliot asked us to make a few revisions in the manuscript we submitted. I went over to London and met the great man himself in 'Uncle Tom's cabin' in Faber's, then in Russell Square. He was fatherly and encouraging. He accepted our revised selection and the anthology, *Contemporary Irish Poetry*, appeared in 1949. Val and I had concocted a fighting introduction, but Eliot dropped it. Here are a few of the unpublished (or unpublishable) sentences:

> Few people really believed that Ireland would succeed in preserving her neutrality: consequently as the problems to be solved in Ireland were similar to those in any other country, it was obvious that it was no use burying one's head under the wool-blanket of the Celtic twilight. Ivory Round Towers, even if complete with the green-whiskered wolfhounds of Banba, Deirdre of the Sorrows, the harp that once and the dying fall of the mellifluous and kingly Gaelic, would hardly provide cover against the assault of tommy-gunned, jack-booted airborne divisions.

Patrick Kavanagh refused to be included in the anthology. Val and I did everything we could except fall on our knees to ensure his inclusion. His peasant stubbornness triumphed. His ploy was to demand a ridiculously high fee that Faber simply refused to give. It was Kavanagh's way of saying no and perhaps hoping for more publicity than if he had been included. A critic in the *New Statesman*, then the most powerful of English weekly reviews, assumed we had left him out for unworthy reasons. I had to write to the paper giving the real facts. Neither Val nor I quarrelled with Paddy because of his obstinacy, but we were bitterly disappointed by his refusal to co-operate.

Frank O'Connor, like Val Iremonger, lived in Sandymount and I went to see him there. He was going through a bitter, irascible phase, and was no doubt angry at being penned up in war-time Ireland.

He had kindly accepted a poem of mine for *The Bell* and written a favourable comment about it as well. When we met, I had no idea of what kind of man he might be—I had only read a few of his short stories in *Guests of the Nation*. He surprised me by the vehemence of his anti-Catholicism, not just his anti-clericalism. Yet he exuded vitality and charm and I came away with a sense of exhilaration. His fellow-Corkman Sean O'Faolain, whom I met about the same time, turned out to be very different: slightly academic but forceful, self-controlled and with an air of sophistication new to me. He took me to tea in a place called Anne's Teashop and I remember one of his questions was "What are young people in Belfast thinking?"

The very first fan letter to come my way was from a lady called Mary Devenport O'Neill whose address was in Kenilworth Square. We began to correspond and I discovered that she herself, middle-aged, was a poet with a volume to her credit and that some of her verse plays had been performed. Her husband, she wrote, was a civil servant in the Department of Education. When I was invited to visit the O'Neills, I called at her husband's office, and he and I went by tram to their home. This proved to be the first of several visits.

The O'Neills lived in a middle-class style unfamiliar to me. I was impressed by the spotless linen tablecloth, the solidly fur-nished and spacious rooms, the silverware, the excellent French wine. Lunch was served by a uniformed maid.

Joseph O'Neill, a tall, ruddy-complexioned man, kept quiet and it was obvious I was his wife's guest. Mrs. O'Neill—she always remained Mrs. O'Neill in those more formal days—turned out to be a lively woman, even a bit confrontational in attitude. She reminisced of the days, evenings rather, when she had run a 'Thursday at Home' attended by famous writers in that very

155

house. Yeats she had known particularly well. She became his consultant when he was writing *A Vision*—a fact recorded in a notebook of Yeats' now in the National Library of Ireland. She told me that Æ (George William Russell)—simple in manner yet a great man and now only dimly recalled by young literary people—used to tease the ageing, somewhat pompous Yeats by calling him 'Willie' and persisting in pronouncing his name as 'Yeets', much to the annoyance of the Nobel prizeman.

Mrs. O'Neill, though naturally influenced by the ideas and ideals of the Celtic Twilight, had wide horizons and was well aware of the work of Proust and Pound, Auden and MacNeice. She felt that Irish writers on the whole were still too concerned with 'the mist that does be on the bog'. This chimed with my own view and she urged me to say so in public.

Joseph O'Neill remained silent while this discussion was in progress, but later he counselled caution saying that a young man ought not to antagonise his elders by being too opinionated. But I, being young and foolish and outspoken in the northern fashion and emboldened by the impulsive Mrs. O'Neill, not to mention the two glasses of Châteauneuf du Pape, paid no heed to this advice. I wrote a fiery letter to the *Irish Times* that resulted in acrimonious replies from the Dublin *literati*. On the other hand, my attack on the old-fashioned literary moulds, drew applause from some of my own contemporaries in Dublin.

Some years were to pass before I began to realise that Joseph O'Neill was himself a significant writer and a man of intellectual distinction. O'Neill, born in Tuam Co. Galway, in 1878, spent his boyhood on the Aran Islands. His upbringing in a house where Irish was spoken made him keenly interested in the revival of the language and its literature so that, after graduating from Queen's College, Galway, he became a student at Kuno Meyer's School of Irish Learning. Later he studied at the University of Freiburg in Germany where he formed a close friendship with Oscar Bergin.

At the age of thirty he gave up his Irish studies to become an inspector of primary schools and, in the same year, married

156

Mary Devenport—also from Galway—who had been a student at the National College of Art. In 1933, he was appointed Secretary of the Department of Secondary Education, a post he held until he retired in 1944.

O'Neill's literary career started with poems in the *Freeman's Journal* and articles in the *Irish Statesman*. It was probably the association with men such as Æ, Yeats, Lennox Robinson and Austin Clarke on those Thursday evenings in Rathgar that led him to attempt more ambitious projects. Five novels with London imprints were to appear, the first in 1934 and the last in 1947.

His *Land Under England* is a political and psychological allegory of a young Englishman caught in a horrifying world under the Yorkshire countryside. This turns out to be an area where the inhabitants are non-human automatons descended from the last Roman soldiers to occupy England. It is a fascinating novel in the tradition of Aldous Huxley's *Brave New World* and the science fiction of H.G. Wells. In 1935, when it appeared, it had relevance to the rise of Hitler and the Nazi attempt to conquer Europe. Æ wrote a preface to *Land Under England* in which he claimed that O'Neill had "elevated the thriller into literature". Æ went on:

... how was I to know for all the torrent of picturesque speech and prodigality of humour, that, within that long head and long body, there were other creatures than those he exposed to me? ... How was I to know that he had it in him to imagine and write *Land Under England* ...?

For a time, I assisted Peadar O'Donnell when he took over the editorship of *The Bell* from O'Faolain. I was the successor to H.A.L. Craig, whom everyone knew as Harry, a big fellow with an enormous shock of fair hair. Harry, the son of a Church of Ireland rector, lived for years in rooms at Trinity, though I think he left without a degree. He used the college as a convenient and relatively cheap place to live. I remember that, outside his door, there stood a vast array of milk bottles that had not been washed out. He was full of energy and used much of it in speaking and canvassing for the Labour Party. Sometimes he would hand me a galley proof for *The Bell* in the Trinity dining hall and ask me to read it for errors. I found Peadar a most erratic employer but a very pleasant one—one could keep whatever office hours one liked. Peadar was a marvellous speaker, both in public and private. He was full of ideas and plans that sounded absolutely convincing. His defect was that he lacked the patience to carry most of them through. Had he been able to do so, I think his impact on Irish public life would have been enormous. His own literary work is significant, all the more so since he split his time between writing and political activism.

It would be tedious to list the various writers and artists I got to know in Dublin (Nano Reid was one of the painters I knew fairly well, though at the time her talent was only beginning to be recognised). The White Stag Group, as they called themselves, were people who had come to Ireland to avoid being involved in the war in England—one of these, Nick Nicholls, painted and wrote poems. A poem by Nicholls, 'The Bone and the Flower', led to controversy when it appeared in *The Bell*. Its symbolism was taken to be sexual and, in the middle 1940s, anything that even hinted at sex came under suspicion. The poem began :

Wound in the seed, the rose's tongue,
Among flowers, the chatter of light and shade ...

Sexual in tone or not, there seemed to me to be a good deal of Edith Sitwell's influence in it.

Pearse Hutchinson, then beginning his career, was a friend of a friend of mine who came from Armagh. Sam Harrison and I met Pearse a few times but never got to know him well. He must have been in touch to some extent over the years, as I have a postcard from him from the International Labour Office building in Geneva. I expect he was visiting Sam in Switzerland where

Sam spent many years. Pearse's inscription runs:

> Friedrich Hölderlin
> hated committing sin,
> but, although he never
>   visited a bad house,
> he still ended up in a madhouse.

The publication of my second volume of poems, *The Undying Day*, in 1948, brought me my first experience of betrayal—at least as an adult. A northern Protestant, whom I considered a friend, attacked it bitterly in a Dublin newspaper to the astonishment of those who knew us both. For some time my wife, Patricia Hutchins, and I had been thinking of leaving for London. It was difficult to make a living in Dublin from freelance writing and occasional part-time jobs in publishing. The day after the review appeared I said to Patricia, "Let's go". Val Iremonger used to say that Belfast was a good place to have come *from*. Dublin seemed to me to have been a good place to have lived *in*. London appeared to be the right place go *to*. I was still following a dream.

SEVENTEEN

Encounters with Kavanagh

In 1942, I was living in Belfast but managed to get a travel permit
to visit London where literary life, somewhat fragmented, still
went on. Stephen Spender had published a poem of mine in
Horizon, of which he was poetry editor. *Horizon*, started by Cyril
Connolly, was, perhaps, the most notable magazine to keep the
cultural flag flying during the war. Spender kindly invited me to
stay in his flat in Maresfield Gardens. One day he said, "Do you
want to meet Connolly?" Something of a rhetorical question. He
went to the phone and arranged that I should present myself at
the *Horizon* offices.

Connolly, as ugly a man as I ever saw, made a few clever,
flippant remarks in keeping with the style of his *Horizon* editori-
als. I was constrained as I had not been with Spender, aware of
being a provincial. He asked if I knew John Hewitt. I said I did.
Then he went to the shelves, loaded with review books despite
the war-time shortage of paper, cloth and skilled printers.

He handed me a copy of Patrick Kavanagh's *The Great Hunger*
which had come out in a Cuala Press limited edition. "Five
hundred words," he said. Before we parted, he asked me, "What
should a writer aim at?" I mumbled something about telling the
truth but sensed that this was not the right answer. "He should
aim at writing a masterpiece," said Connolly. I went out into
London's bomb-scarred streets pleased and chastened.

160

I can still recall the excitement with which, in the Liverpool boat train, I opened the elegant little book in its blue binding and read: "Clay is the word and clay is the flesh ..." It was clear even to a twenty-one year old that a harsh but vital new wind was blowing from County Monaghan, a part of Ulster I knew well. Vivid in memory were those summer holidays I had spent with relatives near Castleblayney.

The stony fields and the people who sweated in them came before my eyes as I read and re-read Kavanagh's masterpiece. The cruel narrowness and frustrations of these small farmers—peasants indeed, though they would have resented the name—seemed real as people in books seldom were. This was raw, disturbing work, quite different from the handful of lyrical and pastoral poems by Kavanagh I had come across. It was different by far from the essentially urban and middle-class attitude of Irish poets of the time. It hit some nerve untouched by, say, Joseph Campbell or F.R. Higgins. Yet powerful as *The Great Hunger* seemed to me, I did make one or two minor criticisms of it in the *Horizon* review.

It was rumoured that the gardaí had confiscated copies of the book and threatened the author with prosecution. I never discovered whether this was a fact or just one of those stories that mushroomed in Dublin pub mythology. But I searched diligently through the poem for lines that might have caused the gardaí to think that poets were as dangerous as parachutists. Was it the veiled reference to masturbation that set off alarm bells?

He sinned over the warm ashes and his crime
The law's long arm could not serve with 'time'.

Were the respectable Civic Guards acting on instructions from still more respectable members of the Catholic *bourgeoisie* outraged by some image like this?

Maguire spreads his legs over the impotent cinders
That wake no manhood now.

As I wrote my *Horizon* review, much exercised by Connolly's parting shot that the aim of a writer was to produce a masterpiece—but were mere reviews exempt from Connolly's Law?—I hoped I would be able to convey something of my excitement to the magazine's mainly English—and sophisticated—readers, who would be unlikely to have any knowledge of the *mores* of the small farmers of County Monaghan. I myself, city-bred and a Protestant at that, had had only fleeting contacts with the people about whom Kavanagh wrote.

I said—here I quote—that *The Great Hunger* was "a poem well worth reading both for its value as poetry, which is simple and direct, and its value as clinical evidence, complex and indirect". I suppose I had picked up the word 'clinical' from W.H. Auden. I had a few reservations as to the poem's value, however, and later was to learn that the notice was not nearly enthusiastic enough for Kavanagh, though he never once referred to it during the several years I knew him. He felt aggrieved, perhaps, that Connolly, in whose prestigious magazine he had published a section of the poem, should have commissioned a review from a young Protestant 'eejit' from the Black North, instead of from some established English critic whose word would carry weight. It is possible that Connolly was intent on a bit of mischief.

It was my witty fellow-Belfastman, the journalist H.L. ('Larry') Morrow—sometimes unkindly nicknamed 'To-morrow'—who introduced me to Kavanagh in the Pearl Bar. Kavanagh greeted me with his native caution, but a torrent of abuse—and here he could be devastating—did not descend on the shy young man who had done his best to be scrupulously fair. On subsequent meetings—realising that I did not bark or bite and rarely argued with my seniors—our relationship thawed into more than acquaintanceship, if a trifle less than friendship. I doubt whether friendship came easily to Kavanagh. Life had taught him to be on his guard.

He and I never met by arrangement, but central Dublin is small and compact, and in those less crowded days we would bump into each other in Bewley's coffee house or in a bar or just

162

in the street. He used to prowl round the streets like a hungry wolf and get especially restless before the evening papers appeared. Paddy, as I soon came to call him, devoured news of all kinds—politics, racing, gossip. For him, the world had dwindled into a parish not unlike his own native Inniskeen. He wanted to know the latest titbit about Churchill or Roosevelt—one of his poems is about Roosevelt—or Hitler, though his own world now seemed confined to the writers and journalists he consorted with in and around the Grafton Street-O'Connell Street area, and to whom he reacted strongly, positively and negatively. His usual greeting to me was, "Hello, Rob, what's new?"

From time to time, as our acquaintance grew, he would call me a "Protestant bastard". This would have been offensive from anyone else, but he would say the words in affectionate tones, almost as if he envied my background. It was a signal that he liked me, for he had a ready stock of vulgar phrases to describe some impeccable Catholic bards who had incurred his wrath! A careless word, a tone of voice, could irritate him. I think his over-sensitivity must have lost him much goodwill. One of Paddy's often repeated tags of abuse was "an ould bags".

So far as Austin Clarke was concerned, I think Kavanagh distrusted rather than hated him. Clarke at that time, a grey eminence in a black hat, had not fulfilled his early promise and nobody could guess at the important work that lay ahead. On the occasions when I met Clarke, he struck me as unhappy and frustrated, fed up with the literary hack work he was forced to do for a meagre living. In the period I am talking about, writers could not travel easily outside Ireland. Censorship laid its dead hand on creativity, the reactionary element in the Catholic Church held sway and it was exceedingly difficult for writers to break into the British or American market. All that contributed to the despondency of Clarke, Kavanagh and others, and was partly responsible for their irritability and willingness to attack each other on the slightest pretext.

The name Brendan Behan I first heard from Kavanagh's lips. They had once been friends. Kavanagh denied this in a court case for libel which he lost and in which the *Leader* magazine was vindicated for its profile of him. The counsel for the defence, Costello, had confronted Kavanagh with a copy of one of his books affectionately inscribed to Brendan, who had done some house-painting for him. By the time Kavanagh talked to me of Behan, their days of friendship were over and he described Behan in picturesque language. Among other things Behan was a "drunken bowsie". The name Behan stuck in my mind. In a few years' time that name was to be known throughout the English-speaking world.

Sometimes I would see Kavanagh strolling along Lower Baggot Street or Grafton Street, stopping to gaze at shop windows, accompanied by a young man called Arthur to whom he talked in a kindly tone. Arthur, whoever he was—and no description of his background was ever forthcoming—uttered not a word. Arthur's clothes and demeanour suggested a middle-class provenance. Could he have been the off-spring of some benefactor?

At other times, I would run into Kavanagh and his brother Peter who taught at a Christian Brothers' school. The two of them occasionally lunched at the Trinity College buffet. Trinity College itself, of course, had been blacklisted for Catholics by the Archbishop of Dublin, Dr. McQuaid, though a sizeable number of Catholic students defied the ban. Peter's ideas and opinions seemed almost identical with Patrick's. At the time, I think he was engaged in research on the Irish theatre for a PhD. He had the education, Paddy had the genius. Peter, too, was combative but could be a pleasant enough fellow when in high good humour. I used to speculate as to whether Peter bore the relationship to Patrick that Stanislaus Joyce did to his elder brother, James.

I would sometimes ask one of the pair "Where's your brother?" only to get the off-hand answer "How do I know?", as if to suggest that the bond between them was not strong. My impression was that, even if the two brothers had a falling out from time to time—as seemed likely—each was highly defensive of the other. Indeed, since Patrick's death, Peter seems to have devoted much of his time and money to re-publishing his brother's prose and poetry. I contributed a short memoir to Peter's life of the poet.

In the preface to Kavanagh's *The Complete Poems*, Peter writes a letter to the dead Patrick:

A year or two ago I might have discussed your funeral, trying to decide which group was the most offensive, those who came or those who stayed away. There were a few genuine friends in attendance, of course ... Much talk of you since you have gone—at least half of it bitter and the remainder begrudging. Still, I suppose one should not complain. Perhaps they mean well. It is hard to say.

Peter Kavanagh goes on to say he has "been whacking away on my own", publishing Patrick's papers, beginning, as arranged between them, with their correspondence, *Lapped Furrows*, followed by *November Haggard*, a selection of uncollected prose.

Peter complains that, for *The Complete Poems* and the other books, not a penny was contributed by anyone but himself— "and this in a world of Cultural Committees, Arts Councils, fellowships and the rest". He recalls that when, in 1952, Patrick asked him if he would help in starting a journal he (Peter) "threw everything I owned into *Kavanagh's Weekly,* knowing I would never see it again". He adds, rather sadly, "I am merely stating the position so that you may know the way things stand— not much different, I'd say, from when you were around". This preface makes for melancholy reading. That a poet of Kavanagh's stature should be neglected is scandalous. Yet there may be another side to it all—simply that Patrick and Peter Kavanagh, hurt by the slings and arrows of the world of Irish letters, turned savagely on their critics. I am confident that a younger generation, both in Ireland and elsewhere, will assess Patrick Kavanagh on his achievement as poet and, to a lesser extent, prose remembrancer of the Monaghan years.

He was a big, shambling creature—a Dr. Johnson, as it were, reincarnated as the son of a small farmer and cobbler in Mucker,

Inniskeen, County Monaghan. Money problems oppressed him as they did Johnson. City slickers patronised him. A countryman to his dying day, Kavanagh fitted uneasily into urban life, yet many years spent in Dublin with some brief excursions to London made him unwilling to return to what we glibly call his 'roots'. A displaced person, he enjoyed his role as a character, and his loud, husky, south Ulster voice boomed dogmatically on subjects large and small. He inveighed against writers who had been formally educated or had made reputations he considered inflated. It did not surprise me to know that Robert Farren, the poet he despised most, put much emphasis on metre and grammar. Kavanagh would have loved to have been present when Dylan Thomas remarked sarcastically, in a room full of American professors, "Isn't education wonderful!"

Kavanagh surprised me one day by appearing at breakfast at the guest house I was staying at. This was an establishment run by a Mrs. Kenny at 19 Raglan Road in Ballsbridge. Here he remained for perhaps six months. It was a somewhat genteel place and peaceful but for the eager bells of the near-by Church of Ireland, which shrilled out even the quarter hours. (One thinks of how maddened Ezra Pound had been by the bells of St. Mary Abbots in Kensington, pre-First World War.) Kavanagh, as might be expected, enjoyed outraging the residents. He would clump into the dining room as if he were returning from footing turf in a bog, march heavily as far as possible from the others—schoolteachers, clerks, students, a violinist in the Radio Eireann orchestra—and, without a word, open a newspaper noisily. Friendly to me outside, he usually ignored me in the house. I tried to stick up for him, but the teachers and sales reps refused to believe that such a man could be a poet, let alone a significant one. They refused to condone his breaking of the conventions. Fifty-odd years ago, doing one's own thing aroused hostility.

Raglan Road apparently came to have an emotional resonance for Kavanagh. One of the loveliest poems in *The Complete Poems* is called 'On Raglan Road' to be sung to the air, 'The Dawning of the Day'. The first quatrain runs:

On Raglan Road on an autumn day I met her first and knew
That her dark hair would weave a snare that I might one day
rue;
I saw the danger, yet I walked along the enchanted way,
And I said, let grief be a fallen leaf at the dawning of the day.

In a note, Peter Kavanagh writes:

> This ballad, originally published in *The Irish Press* under the
> title 'Dark Haired Miriam Ran Away', was written about
> Patrick's girlfriend Hilda but to avoid embarrassment he used
> the name of my girl-friend in the title.

Stories about Kavanagh abounded during the 1940s when I
knew him. They have been embroidered and grow more colourful as time passes. One I remember hearing was his alleged
remark to the editor of *The Standard*, a Catholic weekly in Dublin
(it employed Kavanagh as film critic) on the death of a bishop.
Kavanagh was reputed to have said, "Now the ould bastard
knows there is no God". Yet Kavanagh, in my presence, again
and again emphasised his belief in God and in Mother Church,
and his contempt for atheists and agnostics. He liked to shock,
so the story about the bishop may well be true. He would not
listen to a 'dirty story' much less tell one. He liked women to be
what then was called 'womanly' and remarked of a girl friend of
mine that she was "a real woman". No higher praise could he
give. As for poets then writing, the only one I heard him
commend without reservation was W.H. Auden. He kept quiet
about Yeats whom he probably thought more 'Anglo' than Irish
and given too high a place in the pantheon. Val Iremonger and
I asked him repeatedly to let us represent him in our Faber
anthology, *Contemporary Irish Poetry* (1949). He made various
excuses, one of them being that the fee offered was not high
enough. For whatever reason—and we guessed that the real
reason was that he wanted undue representation—he does not

167

appear in it, more's the pity. I think he had the faintest touch of snobbery, to judge from various remarks. He spoke kindly of Harold Macmillan whom he had met at the family firm of publishers in London. "A real gentleman," he called him.

Kavanagh, I believe, liked to consider *himself* "a real gentleman", one who was free of the shams and hypocrisies of the lower middle class, 'the lace curtain Irish' of American usage. That may be why he was so contemptuous of the people in the Ballsbridge guest house. He despised the way they opted for 'correctness', their sheep-like acceptance of the social conventions. He might well have endorsed the D.H. Lawrence of 'How beastly the bourgeois' and execrated 'Willie Wetleg'. I'm sure he would have approved of Frieda von Richtofen as being "a real woman". He hated all establishments, literary, political and ecclesiastical. I was once in a group with him when someone quoted, "Whatever is, is right". Kavanagh in a flash said, "Whatever is, is shite".

Savage indignation lacerated Kavanagh as it lacerated Swift—and, despite his remark about excrement, he had a squeamishness, even prudery, that was a bit Swiftian. He tried to discipline his strong emotions but then out would come some ill-considered remark that caused offence or laughter, according to the company.

Kavanagh's autobiography, *The Green Fool*, published in 1938, must have made him feel on the verge of a breakthrough into literary recognition, but the book had to be withdrawn because of a libel action by Oliver St. John Gogarty. "Stately, plump Buck Mulligan" had taken exception to Kavanagh's remark that the woman who answered his knock on the door had been Gogarty's mistress. As a result, *The Green Fool* did not get back into print until 1971, years after Kavanagh's death. This has not met with the approval of Peter Kavanagh who says, in the preface from which I have already quoted: "Recently *The Green Fool* was re-issued but since you stated many times that this book was part of your juvenilia it is hard to know the motive behind the present edition." However, I am inclined to think that the *Irish Press* reviewer was not so far wrong in writing: "*The Green Fool* has Traherne's mystic vision, Hemingway's stark simplicity, Thurber's fantastic humour; and it is one of the few authentic accounts of life in Ireland in this century."

I lost touch with Paddy Kavanagh when I left Dublin for London in 1948 but the green fool—and genius—remains vivid in my memory. The child or fool in him ensured the freshness, the originality of his writing, its freedom from influence and artificiality.

Some recognition did come to him before he died in 1967, aged 62, after a losing battle with cancer. Anthony Cronin was one of those younger fellow writers who championed him. Fortunately, Kavanagh had a splendid second phase as a poet and I was glad to hear that well on in years he had married—and happily, I hope. When I wonder about his life, as I have often done, speculating on whether it contained more misery than happiness, I keep remembering that he wrote, "Great poetry is always comic in the profound sense". He echoed W.B. Yeats who believed in an ultimate gaiety. Kavanagh was much more than a local poet, a parochial poet, yet it is hard not to identify him with his early years in Monaghan where his native black hills forever look north towards Armagh as he tells us in 'Shancoduff':

My hills hoard the bright shillings of March
While the sun searches in every pocket.
They are my Alps and I have climbed the Matterhorn
With a sheaf of hay for three perishing calves
In the field under the Big Forth of Rocksavage.

Would he, I wonder, have been less the poet he is if he had never looked south, first to Dublin and then to London? Would he have been a happier man?

EIGHTEEN

Never go back, boy!

'Whenever you go back to any place,' she said and I marvelled at the phrase, 'across the planets of the years, nothing is the way it was when you were young. Never go back, girl.'
—Sean O'Faolain, 'The Planets of the Years'

When I return from time to time to the damp Belfast streets of childhood and youth and early manhood, they no longer glitter like patent leather. They are sleazier, more littered. The lights are less bright. All changed, if not changed utterly. And not just because of the 'troubles', which have brought destruction and tragedies too frequent to record to Belfast and the six counties. Even before the latest outbreak of civil strife, the process of change was well under way—flyovers, blocks of flats, new hotels, high rises, fast food, Chinese restaurants. Even so, many of the old buildings still remain intact if put to different uses. My aunts' newsagent's shop on the Stranmillis Road is still a newsagent's shop.

The vivid faces of the generation before mine have all gone—mother, father, Aunt Tillie, Uncle George, Tommy Gibson. All dead as, indeed, are some of my contemporaries, one or two of them younger than myself. I walk, a kind of exile, in a city of ghosts. As my late friend, the poet and writer, Clifford Dyment, put it:

The end is death!
I cry in terror.
In the end, death,
Agrees the mirror.

Ghosts—and memories. An image that comes to mind is of a doorway in Royal Avenue, a short distance from the Grand Central Hotel. It was a war-time evening, with army officers and their girlfriends coming and going to and from the hotel. I had been bored and depressed. Life seemed to consist wholly of blackout and drizzle. I went into a scruffy, ill-lit cafe somewhere around Rosemary Street. There I got into a bantering conversation with a buxom, dark-skinned girl called Peggy who wore gipsy ear-rings and had been unsparing in the use of powder and rouge. She spoke in that harsh type of local accent that lends itself to easy mimicry and laughter. I felt we could continue our conversation in a less oppressive atmosphere.

"Would you like a drink ?" I asked, a trifle apprehensively, for I carried in my mind the idea of the Demon Drink.

"Well, I've never had one before," Peggy replied, "but I don't mind if you don't mind." We went out into the drizzle and searched for a bar.

For a girl who had never had a drink before, Peggy showed a remarkable capacity as a learner. She consumed several gin-and-limes with consummate ease. I drank a couple of bottles of Guinness and felt well on the way down the slippery path. The dark brew went slightly to my head. Peggy told me about her dear old granny up the Crumlin Road and how careful she had to be "with all them Yank soldiers about". She surprised me by telling me she hated the police. This, in our small, in-grown community, signalled the fact that Peggy did not belong to my own tribe.

After our drinks we went out and, without speaking, looked for a doorway around Smithfield. The streets were unpeopled in the black night, all solid citizens were at home listening to the radio and drinking cocoa. Peggy kissed me with abandon and

171

pulled me vigorously towards her. I arranged to meet the dark-locked Peggy a few days later, thinking she might assuage the ache in my heart Irene had caused. We were to meet in the pub. I arrived punctually but, after a few minutes, I had a feeling she would not turn up. I drank glass after glass of the dark beer as I waited—in vain.

Two or three weeks later, I did catch a glimpse of Peggy. She was strolling along arm-in-arm with a soldier—an American private, First Class. I accepted my defeat with philosophic calm. After all, Peggy was no Irene, no inspirer of high endeavour, no Beatrice for a would-be Dante. Hundreds of Peggies roamed the streets, hardly distinguishable one from another. In the whole wide, mad, cruel world there was but one Irene.

Irene, goddess of peace, had been a symbol of light in a dark and threatening world. The flesh-and-blood person who once existed for me becomes less and less real as the years blur the image. Have not most of us, one way and another, had an Irene in our lives? She is the girl we once saw in a train and loved instantly, but never even spoke to. She is the person we have lost. For poets and dreamers, because they trade in images and magic, the Irenes, the Maud Gonnes, are not so much women as enchantresses.

In 'Poetry and Truth', Goethe tells of his Irene who, in actual fact, was called Gretchen. He says:

It was at this time, too, that a friend urgently invited me to an evening party ... We met quite late; the meal was most frugal, the wine just drinkable ... When at last the latter gave out someone called for a servant. Instead there appeared a girl of uncommon and, indeed, in that environment, of incredible beauty.

'What do you want?' she asked, after she had saluted us all in the friendliest way. 'The maid servant is ill and in bed. Perhaps I can help you.'

'There's no wine left,' said one of the company. 'If you were to get us a couple of bottles, it would be very nice.'

'Oh please do, Gretchen,' said another. 'It's only three steps' ...

From that moment on the image of this girl followed me wherever I went. It was the first lasting impression which a being of the other sex had made on me. Since I could neither find nor even seek a pretext to see her in her house, I attended church for her sake. I soon found out where she would sit and so I gazed my fill during the long Protestant service ...

The first stirrings of love of an unspoiled youth take on a decisive spiritual collaboration. Nature seems to desire that one sex should apprehend in the other that which is good and beautiful in sensuous form. And so to me, too, there was revealed through the vision of this girl and through my love of her a new world of the beautiful and the excellent.

For Irene's sake, I too—so recently a devout young Leftist and rebel against religious authority of all kinds—attended services at the virginally-white Christian Science Church near the University. Like Goethe on his Gretchen, I too gazed my fill on Irene during the long service.

Illusions, delusions, romantic will-o'-the-wisps die hard. When I go back home—ah, but is it *really* home any longer?—I still on solitary evening strolls keep an eye out for the figure of slender, willowy Irene. Whether she is alive or dead or, if alive, where she may live, I do not know. Perhaps I am still following a dream. And I think of the youth who, half a century ago, eased his heartache by writing

Sorrow for everything, and not knowing
Why it matters so much.

Also by Robert Greacen
from Lagan Press

Robert Greacen
Collected Poems 1944-1994

ISBN: 1 873687 55 9
174 pp, £5.95 pbk

For fifty years Robert Greacen has been one of the most
quietly distinctive voices in Irish poetry. From the political
and aesthetic intensities of the neo-Romantic
One Recent Evening (1944) and *The Undying Day* (1948),
the ironic, urbane and self-knowing satires of
A Garland for Captain Fox (1975) and *Young Mr. Gibbon* (1979),
to the autobiographical celebrations and elegies of his
northern upbringing in *Carnival at the River* (1990), he has
followed his own course outside the modes of poetic fashion.
Yet unifying the poems is a belief in poetry and its ceaseless
engagement with the self and the social world.

Gathering together all of his poetic output to the present day,
Robert Greacen: Collected Poems 1944-1994 stands as a testimony
to a unique sensibility in contemporary Irish poetry.

"Greacen's is a voice that has been given too little heed
in his native country. The poems run the gamut—one might
almost say the gauntlet—of human emotions and respond
with the subtlest of sardonic satire, with the most suavely
debonair urbanity and with an honesty and sincerity
that are totally disarming."
—Conleth Ellis

"It is with shrewd observation, a fine Swiftian wit
and considerable poetic control that Greacen views
a modern society inhabited by ordinary people. He writes
with an immediacy that is much sought after these days."
—Martin Booth